Homer White

The Norwich Cadets

A Tale of the Rebellion

Homer White

The Norwich Cadets
A Tale of the Rebellion

ISBN/EAN: 9783337073961

Printed in Europe, USA, Canada, Australia, Japan

Cover: Foto ©ninafisch / pixelio.de

More available books at **www.hansebooks.com**

THE NORWICH CADETS:

A

TALE REBELLION.

By REV. HOMER WHITE,

AUTHOR OF "THE CAPTIVE BOY," ETC.

---•◆•---

ST. ALBANS, VT
PUBLISHED BY ALBERT CLARKE,
1873.

THE NORWICH CADETS.

CHAPTER I.

INTRODUCTORY.

THE only military school of which Vermont can boast, or ever could boast, with the exception of that peripatetic school in which Ethan Allen and Seth Warner were professors, is Norwich University.

It is worthy of note that after any war the people who have been engaged in it evince a decided taste for military knowledge. After the occasion has passed which called for such knowledge, they set about perfecting themselves in the art of war. In their fresh ardor they found military schools and organize volunteer regiments with a patriotic determination to be prepared for the next struggle. But after a while men get tired of drilling, and as the quiet time of peace is prolonged they lose their interest in martial show, and the next war in which they are called to engage finds them again a nation of shopkeepers and farmers, equally ignorant of military tactics and of the principles and practice of gunnery. Such was eminently our situation at the beginning of the late rebellion. At its close, when the danger was past, we began, according to this tendency of nature which I have spoken of, to beat our pruning hooks into

spears and to learn war some more. Now, in consequence
of this and of our late experience in war, we are as a people
fairly versed in military science, but probably by the
time we shall need this knowledge it will be numbered
among our lost acquirements.

Norwich University was the product of the *post bellum*
fever induced by our last war with Great Britain. It was
established in the year 1820. Though now located at North-
field, it was first and for many years in the town and village
of Norwich, on the Connecticut river and opposite Hanover,
N. H., the seat of Dartmouth College. The river flowed
between the two institutions of learning, but they were
less than a mile distant from each other. The first head of
the University was Capt. A. Partridge. Its course of study
embraced more than the college curriculum generally does,
and if its graduates became thoroughly proficient in one
half of the things they were expected to learn, they left its
walls accomplished soldiers. The institution soon became
popular and flourishing, and attracted pupils from nearly
every State in the Union.

Norwich has furnished some names for the roll of fame
—names of which Vermont is and ever will be proud.
High among these stands that of the gallant Ransom, who
was at one time president of the University, and who lost
his life at the beginning of a glorious career in the war
with Mexico.

At the time at which our story opens, 1859, the University.
with its veteran brick walls somewhat weather-beaten,
stood as the most prominent object in the quiet village of
Norwich. There were only about forty cadets, of all class-
es at the University, for the reason that the country had
enjoyed a long interval of peace, and a knowledge of Har-
dee's Tactics was not considered the most valuable sort of
information for a young man to possess in beginning the
campaign of life. Had our prudent countrymen foreseen

the nearness of the rebellion, the University would doubtless have been crowded with martial youth in search of martial knowledge.

Most of the cadets were Green Mountain boys though there were some from distant states, but all were youths so full of war instinct that the most profound peace could not banish their dreams of war. No dress seemed to them so beautiful as the army blue; burnt powder had a delightful odor: and the roar of guns and the rattle of drums were music to their ears.

There are such men everywhere, born soldiers, who have an innate scorn of peaceful pursuits, and long for the clash of arms and the din of battle; who leave the plow field for the "field of honor" with all the alacrity of Putnam, though without half the cause; men who make war, if they do not find it, like the fierce son of the shrinking Werner in Byron's tragedy. Fallen man in a state of nature is not the simple, inoffensive creature which Rousseau makes him, but a blood-thirsty animal delighting in carnage. He makes war upon all other creatures, though not to satisfy the demands of hunger, and even destroys those of his own kind for the mere pleasure of shedding blood.

At the same time brave men who have a passion for arms and who glory in battle, often possess some of the noblest traits of character. Their virtues light up some pages of the dark history of war and conquest, and make their battles something better than the struggles of brutes or the strifes of fiends.

Though civilization, in its refining process, has taken the courage out of most of us, we have still enough of savage nature left in us to feel a genuine admiration for courage in others. Though we may be disinclined to adventure our own lives by walking into a forest of bayonets, even for the most righteous cause, yet the most cowardly of us all respect the brave man and admire his gallant deeds.

"Peace hath her victories no less than war," but peace is tame and humdrum. War has charms of a more exciting character, and the bare recital of its deeds has power to accelerate the pulse of the most determined Quaker. We read the war chapters of a nation's history with the greatest gusto, and we delight in the military achievements of the world's heroes from Ulysses of Ithaca to Ulysses of Galena.

During the late civil war Norwich University sent a larger proportion of her graduates into the field than did any other college in the country. And she furnished for the volunteer army five Major Generals, twenty-seven Colonels and a large number of officers of lower grade. They did valiant service for their country, and we believe that in reading some of their adventures and in recalling some of the events of the great struggle for the Union, we shall be doing no more than justice to the heroism of our gallant State, while we incite in our readers a deeper love of their country and a more chivalrous devotion to its honor. We may not convince them all that it is sweet to die for one's country, but they will at least feel that the honors showered upon the head of the patriot-soldier are honors well deserved.

In 1859 the Rev. Dr. Bournes was President of Norwich and had been so for ten years. He was a man of peace by profession and as well versed in canon law as in cannon balls. It may seem strange that a military academy should have a clerical head, but it is perhaps well to maintain an equilibrium of forces. There was plenty of latent fire among the cadets and they were ready at any time to explode, like so many cans of nitro-glycerine; but the cassock generally kept the mastery of the Cossack, and the science of war was peacefully pursued. Certain it is that the boys would as soon have thought of bearding "the Douglass in his hall" as the "Doctor" in his study.

But the strictest order did not always reign in the barracks, nor was it always quiet on the Connecticut. From time immemorial, that is to say from the foundation of the University, a feud had raged between the cadets and the students of Dartmouth college across the river, and many raids and encounters had taken place, in regard to which and the heroes engaged in them, tradition had much to say. The cadets were inferior in numbers to their classical antagonists, but they were filled with martial ardor and utterly unwilling to admit that the stylus is mightier than the sword. The prevailing opinion among them seemed to be that Dartmouth must be destroyed. The discipline of the University prevented the attempt, by any well organized expedition, to accomplish this favorite object, but it was not sufficient to restrain individual cadets from hostile incursions into the enemy's country. Bristling with daggers and revolvers which they never had a serious thought of using, two or three together would cross the river at night, either by the bridge or by boat, and parade the streets of Hanover or penetrate even to "Tempe's pleasant vale" with a marked disregard of the dangers they incurred. Frequently they succeeded in provoking hostilities, and then they displayed the gallantry which afterward distinguished them upon larger fields. When greatly outnumbered, as they usually were, they would fall back to the river with a celerity to which Xenophon's famous retreat furnishes no parallel. If they found the bridge disputed they took to boats, or if these were not to be found, a flank movement, up or down the river to a fording place, was executed in a masterly manner, and the barracks gained sometime before reveille. The casualties were always few, but the fun and glory were considerable.

CHAPTER II.

TOM AND BILL—HOSTILITIES WITH DARTMOUTH STUDENTS—MAT CONDON'S NAVAL ENGAGEMENT.

OUR two heroes, who were chums and inseparable companions, were known and always designated by their fellow cadets as Tom and Bill. They were from different sections of the Union, and the opposites of each other in personal appearance. They had been born and reared in very different circumstances and could hardly be expected to have much sympathy the one with the other, or to care for a very close fellowship; but the strong bond of union between them was the unshrinking courage and love of adventure which each perceived and appreciated in the other. They were, as we have said, inseparable companions, and they were also devoted friends.

Tom Lyon was the son of a Vermont farmer and accustomed to labor with his hands without being at all ashamed of it. He was of the Anglo-Saxon type, brown hair, blue eyes and fair skin. Though only of medium height he was compactly built, with muscles like bundles of whip-cord, and by far the strongest man at the University. This fact coupled with another, equally well-known, that he had never been seen to exhibit fear even in the most trying situations, won for him the hearty respect and admiration of those who reverence physical strength and courage. But he had other and more worthy claims to respect; his classical attainments were not inferior to those of the average "junior" on the other side of the river; he had strong convictions of right, was honorable and high minded, patriotic and true. His word could not be justly questioned and never was with impunity. Confidence reposed in him was a sacred trust, never betrayed, and taken altogether he was a noble specimen of the Green Mountain Boy. He was, however, still a boy, not yet twenty-one, and with the animation of youth he had also some of its follies.

Bill or William Wolfe, our other hero, was the son of a Georgia planter and brought up in aristocratic idleness. He was of slender form, with dark hair and eyes and swarthy complexion. There was a strain of Spanish blood in his veins and he had that adventurous and chivalrous disposition which distinguished the conquerors of Mexico and Peru. Restless, and always longing for change of scene and excitement, his wealthy and indulgent father had permitted him to rove at will, insisting only that he should at least make a pretence of seeking an education; and he had been an inmate of several Northern as well as Southern schools and colleges, acquiring in his perigrinations a considerable fund of book-knowledge together with much other information. At Norwich his liberality and his various accomplishments, among which was skill in the use of arms and of the less deadly gloves, quickly made him a favorite among the cadets and introduced him to the favor and friendship of Tom Lyon. With a nice sense of honor and a haughty temper, he was easily offended, and then there was observable a nervous twitching about the eyes and a growing blackness of the face which betokened mischief. Very quick in his movements, much stronger than he appeared to be, and recklessly brave, he was an antagonist not lightly to be encountered. There was no one at the University who could meet him with any chance of success, with the ex ception of his sworn friend Tom Lyon. And in this case it was the superior strength of the North, and that alone, which could overcome the South.

To say that young Wolfe was not fond of hostile encounters *per se* without regard to the occasion of them, would be untrue; but it would be equally untrue to say that he ever sought a quarrel when the advantage was evidently in his favor. He was too nobly brave to contend with any one plainly weaker than himself. His battles, which were numerous, were always with an enemy superior either in strength or numbers, and hence he usually came out of them severely beaten. But no amount of beating could beget in him a love of peace. He was a born controversialist, who chose the sword rather than the pen with which to present his arguments and convince his opponents.

These pictures of our heroes are not fancy sketches, but drawn from a vivid recollection. We may not all approve of such pugnacious characteristics as I have delineated, but we know that they exist, and that there would be many blank pages in history if the record of the events proceeding from such characteristics were to be blotted out. We shall follow our heroes to more noble fields of action than school-boy quarrels, and it will be seen in fiction as it is to be found in fact, that those who love war for war's sake are generally those who excel in it, and that in a righteous cause the instinct for battle becomes an instrument of good.

It was after the arduous duties of a summer's day—recitations, drill and the evening mess—that Tom and Bill sat in what they called their den, leisurely engaged in filling it with smoke which they drew from a couple of pipes. Occasionally they glanced through the blue atmosphere at each other, apparently waiting for a suggestion in regard to what next. Nothing was said by either for some minutes, but before the quiet became painful it was disturbed by the sound of heavy footsteps. Then the door was pushed open without ceremony and in stalked the gigantic and loud voiced cadet, Mat Condon. His name was Martin Van Buren, but it was familiarly abbreviated to Mat. His head towered over six feet aloft and was covered with long shaggy yellow hair, giving him the appearance of a lion rampant. He prided himself upon this appearance and his prodigious strength, and wished to be regarded as another Cœur de Leon. But the lion heart was not in his bosom, and whenever he was brought to the test he was sure to be discovered like the fabled ass in the lion's skin. But he was the poet of the University, and had written and could sing in a roaring manner the song of "the Old South Barracks, O," and being a jolly companion and perfectly harmless in spite of his mammoth proportions, he was patronized by our two heroes and afforded them much amusement.

"Hello! boys, what are you so still for?" cried the newcomer as he planted himself in the centre of the smoke-clouded room, like Mt. Mansfield in a fog.

"Well," replied Tom in his deliberate manner, "as we didn't see any necessity for making a noise, we concluded to spare the exertion."

"My collossal friend," said Bill in his blandest tones, "please moor yourself to that stool and tell us how many men you have killed since breakfast."

"*Diem perdidi!* not even one.

> But a field of the dead rushes red on my sight,
> For the students of Dartmouth are spoiling for fight."

"Now my brave Falstaff with the lion head, give us a prose translation of that," said Tom, "for I see that your big skin is full of something new."

"My dear boy," returned Condon, I grieve for you and I always sing my sorrows. But the fact is, a certain pugnacious sophomore has hurled his gauntlet across the river and expresses a particular desire that you should pick it up."

"Ah! indeed, that is refreshing intelligence. You shall be rewarded."

"Couldn't the gentleman toss over one apiece for us?" inquired Bill, feeling that he had been slighted.

"He thinks that one hand is enough for both of you, and therefore used only one glove."

Bill sprang to his feet at this and buttoning his coat up to the chin, secured about him the silver hilted dagger which he always carried, and began pacing the room cap in hand. The cooler blooded Vermonter smiled at these evidences of excitement, and addressing his chum by the affectionate appellation of "Willie," requested him to have another pipe.

"No, thank you, I have got to throw a pontoon across the Connecticut to-night, so that the Doctor can lead his troops over in the morning to attack the town."

"Wouldn't you accept the services of a couple of volunteers?" inquired Tom.

"Yes."

"Come on then, Condon," said Tom rising and putting on his cap; we shall need you as guide. If it isn't very dark we shall be able to follow your white face without difficulty."

"I am with you my gallant boys," exclaimed the poet, striking an attitude, "till—

"The enemy heaves in sight." Tom finished the sentence.

The three sallied out together and avoiding the guards took their way to the river. As they neared the bridge Condon called a halt.

"I pride myself on my generalship," said he, "and I can't bear to throw away the lives of such good soldiers as you. Now it is very easy to get into Hanover, but when we wish to get out we may find this bridge barricaded. So my beasts of prey, to make our retreat secure, if you will go ahead, I will go and get a boat and row over and wait for you at the landing."

"No head but yours would have thought of that," said Bill.

"Do so by all means," said Tom.

Condon looked pleased that his companions so readily fell in with his plan, which was first conceived to secure his own safety, and walked away with as much energy and importance as though it were the night of crossing the Delaware and upon him rested the responsibility of finding transportation for the troops.

The two friends laughed quietly over this desertion.

"That is the last we shall see of him" remarked Bill.

"Big dogs are not the bravest," philosophized Tom; "but he may come over after all."

"If he starts at all, he is more likely to drop anchor in the middle of the stream where he will be out of harm's reach from either shore."

With another laugh at poor Mat's want of courage and his futile endeavors to conceal it, the two cadets walked on over the bridge and entered the village of Hanover. Without intending to provoke any quarrel, they were determined to let their presence be known, and were prepared to repel any assault, whether made by the pugnacious sophomore before mentioned, or by others. They were personally well known, but not regarded with unmixed love, for the reason that on several former occasions they had difficulties with different students and had generally borne away what laurels there were.

After visiting two or three places of student-resort, they found themselves receiving as much attention as they desired. Their very presence there was a challenge and so received. The excitement momentarily increased. Leaving the refreshment saloon, at that time kept by a colored gentleman who dispensed oysters and root beer to hungry and thirsty undergraduates, the two cadets proceeded to the Campus followed by a noisy and not very respectful crowd. They paid no attention however to those behind them nor to the uncomplimentary remarks which were made for their ears, but walked along unconcernedly as though they were the only persons abroad.

Perceiving that some more decided demonstration must be made, the crowd pressed, closed, and finally the champion of the sophomore class, a tall fellow named Staples, brushing up to Bill's side laid his hand on the Georgian's coat and cried out—

"See! what pretty buttons!"

There was a laugh from his companions, but it quickly subsided as they saw their champion sprawling on the ground, sent there by one quick blow from the insulted cadet. Then they rushed in a body on the now furious southerner.

"One at a time, gentlemen," said Tom cooly, as he knocked down the foremost of the assailants. "My friend will meet any one of you in fair fight."

"Or a dozen of them" cried Bill with a face as black as Othello's.

The battle now became general. The cadets received some hard blows, but they repaid them with interest. Once Bill was down, but Tom fought over his body till he could gain his feet. Doubtless the battle would have gone against our heroes in the end, but suddenly the President of the College appeared in the midst of the combatants, calling excitedly for order.

The students no sooner saw him than they fled to avoid his recognition. The cadets, saluting him respectfully, marched away leaving the astonished President sole occupant and master of the lately contested field.

Our two heroes directed their steps to the river. Soon becoming aware that they were pursued, Bill expressed a desire to turn back, but yielding to his friend's request he hastened with him to the landing where they hoped but hardly expected to find Condon.

That individual had indeed procured a boat and an inoffensive fellow to row it and made a landing on the New Hampshire shore. When he heard the sound of hurrying footsteps and angry shouts he suspected the cause, and fearful of being himself sacrificed if he waited to succor his friends, he jumped into the boat and seizing one oar while his companion took the other, pushed out a few rods into the river just as Tom and Bill reached the shore.

They saw they were too late and running a short distance up the stream secreted themselves. Their pursuers soon after reached the landing they had just left, and seeing a boat with two persons in it, naturally supposed that their foes had escaped them. They shouted after the fleeing Condon, daring him to return, and one of them having a revolver, fired several shots purposely striking the water at a safe distance from the boat.

At this the frightened boatman whom Condon had hired stopped rowing and proposed to return in obedience to the order of the firing party.

"Row for your life" screamed the frantic giant, drawing a huge knife and flourishing it wildly.

"They will shoot us if we don't go back."

"Fear nothing but me. You carry Condon and his fortunes."

The boat sped on its way and the baffled students left the spot.

When all was quiet Tom and Bill emerged from their hiding place, where they had greatly enjoyed the spectacle of Condon's terror, and crossing the bridge unmolested, peacefully pursued their way home.

CHAPTER III.

CONDON'S ADVENTURE—THE BATTLE OF TORN COATS—A POLITICAL DISCUSSION—THE GATHERING STORM.

THE next morning Mat had a wonderful tale to tell of his adventures by flood and field and of the narrow escape from death which he had in contending single handed with the chivalry of Dartmouth. Our two heroes heard his report with interest, and Bill moved that it be engrossed and placed in the archives of the University.

After this affray quiet reigned on the Connecticut for the space of three weeks. But this peace could not continue. The "Darties" (as the Dartmouth students were called) smarted under their late defeat, and only waited for an opportunity to wreak their vengeance on some one or more of the cadets without being at the cost and danger of making a hostile incursion into Vermont for that purpose. This opportunity soon presented itself.

Condon, whose political and martial qualities we have before had occasion to notice, afforded the *casus belli* this time. Not contented with having stolen the title and parodied the favorite song of the cadets called the "old south barracks," a really meritorious production written by Harry Dent, a former cadet: and not satisfied with the many scrapes into which he had been the means of leading his fellow students, was now the "cause, means and instrument" of bringing on what we shall call the last battle of Dartmouth, or the battle of Torn Coats. Trusting to his fear inspiring proportions and appearance, and to a peaceable demeanor, he ventured one Saturday to pass over to Hanover alone and unprotected.

His arrival in the village was quickly known and he was soon the object of almost universal attention. The Darties welcomed this opportunity for revenge, and with Staples at their head surrounded him.

Condon grew pale with fear and all his great strength left him. He tried to look courageous and walk out of the net, but as his reputation was not altogether unknown, they stopped him and laughed at his frowns and hard words. He cried "peace," but they told him there was none; he begged for mercy and they hissed him.

His knees smote together as Staples fiercely approached him. The boys enjoyed his terror. But they were too manly to think of doing any bodily injury to one so completely in their power.

Staples seized him by his claw hammer coat-tails, and deliberately ripped Condon's outer garment up to the collar. That alone held the two halves of the coat together.

With shouts and screams of laughter the "Darties" opened their ranks and permitted the humbled cadet to march out of their midst.

Holding his coat together behind, as well as he could with one hand, Condon fairly ran, followed by peals of laughter which sounded like volleys of artillery in his ears, and stopped not till he was safely on the other side of the river. He tried to gain his room unseen, but in this he failed.

Lyon and Wolfe, who were walking together, met him, and their laughter at his ridiculous appearance seemed to be the echo of that from which he had fled.

"Is that the newest style—the regulation pattern?" inquired the first.

c

"Why don't you move your buttons around if you are going to have your coat open on that side?" said the other.

Poor Condon tried to tell how he had caught his coat on a fence post, but his scared look did not confirm his tale, and he was finally obliged to confess to part of the truth. He told, however, how he had been overpowered by numbers, and after a desperate struggle, he had been abused in the manner they saw.

Though greatly amused at Condon's mishap, the honor of the University was at stake, as our friends thought, and they determined upon retaliation.

The story was told; there was a private meeting of the cadets and to the number of forty-five they agreed that the disgrace should be wiped out.

A neighboring wood-pile was laid under contribution for weapons. They sawed the four foot limbs in two; bored gimlet holes in one end; tied in a loop of small cord and threw the loop over the wrist, as cavalry men wear their swords in action.

This gave each man a neat club of two feet in length with a sword-knot to prevent him from losing it, should it be knocked out of his hand.

With these formidable weapons (similar to a policeman's club) they marched to Hanover, though Condon was not among them. He complained of being unwell, and at the time of departure was snugly tucked up in bed, with numerous bottles of medicine on a stand at his bedside.

When the cadets reached Hanover they drew up on the college green, and forming a hollow square (single rank eleven men on a side), they gave three groans for Dartmouth, followed by three cheers for Norwich University.

They did not have to wait long for the enemy to appear. The Darties swarmed from every direction and assembled on all sides of them.

Among the cadets was an Ohio boy named Evarts

(afterwards a Colonel of Volunteers) whose weight was two hundred and thirty-five pounds and whose strength and courage corresponded well with his weight. A blacksmith's anvil of ordinary size was a toy in his huge hands. When the cadets formed the square under command of Adjutant Lyon, Evarts refused to fall in, and as the Dartmouth men pressed close up, he seized the first who came near him by the shoulders, whirled him around, and tore his coat from skirt to collar. He followed this thing up by treating half a dozen others in the same manner, before hostilities on the part of the square were actually opened.

Lyon marched his little force first in one direction and then in another, wherever the crowd appeared densest, making a path wherever they went. The advantage which the cadets possessed over their antagonists, consisted in their military organization and their consequent ability to strike as a unit against an unorganized mob.

Stones, brickbats and sticks fell among them, but rarely inflicted any serious damage. After a time the fall of missiles slackened; and the attention of the enemy seemed to be drawn toward an opposite section of the green. Lyon seized the opportunity to give his command a breathing spell by ordering an "in place, rest."

The cadets had only drawn a few free breaths, however, when they saw Evarts standing alone with his arms folded, about a hundred feet in front of them, while immediately beyond him stood the Dartmouth host, evidently watching and considering his probable movements, and meditating his overthrow.

Presently two men appeared approaching him from either side; a third came up in front and dared him by gestures; a fourth stole to the rear of Goliah. Evarts sprang for the man in front, and at the same time the three men in flank and rear sprang upon him. The giant went down.

"Tention!" shouted Adjutant Lyon; "forward, double quick!"

In half a minute the square marched over the five struggling men, halted and held them in the center. Evarts sprang to his feet, caught each man singly and ripped up his coat.

"Glory enough for one day! To the Barracks, double quick, march!" exclaimed Lyon, and the cadets ran unmolested down the hill to Vermont, Evarts and Wolfe bringing up the rear and earnestly longing to be pursued.

Their longing was not gratified. They were not pursued, but gained the barracks in safety, and indulged in great rejoicings over their victory.

Condon was visibly better as he heard the news, and the next day appeared as well as ever.

But more important events than these we have described, were in the near future, and were soon to be unfolded not only to the gaze of the cadets, but to the whole country and the world.

The presidential campaign of 1860 was a very exciting one because the people felt that greater interests than usual were involved in it, if indeed the life of the nation was not at stake. And after the election was over, the excitement, instead of subsiding as it usually does after such an event, rather increased. During the winter the threats of secession advocates grew louder and more frequent—the mutterings of the gathering storm burst upon the country with the thunder of the guns directed against Fort Sumter.

In politics Tom and Bill could not agree, but they could do what many older heads cannot do, they could discuss questions about which they differed, without exhibiting any personal animosity or feeling any diminution of their friendship. The Vermonter was a staunch republican and anti-slavery man, a firm supporter of Lincoln, while the Georgian was a Breckinridge democrat and a pro slavery man. The former was a disciple of Webster and believed that "We the people" had granted to the general government greater powers than any that were reserved. The latter was a disciple of Calhoun and believed in state rights. If he must choose between Georgia and the United States, he chose Georgia as having the stronger claim upon his loyalty.

Many a wordy contest did the two cadets have with each other, but prejudice with them as with most men, was stronger than reason, and they usually ended as far apart as when they began.

"Why should not the South have its independence, if it desires it?" inquired Bill. "You believe in the right of revolution."

"In some cases; but I don't believe in treason," answered Tom.

"That is dodging the point. Secession is revolution."

"Governments are instituted among men for the benefit of the governed, and when they become destructive of this end, it is the right of the people to alter or abolish them. So I believe, and I believe that an oppressed people is justified in revolution or secession without a cause. The south claims the right to withdraw at will from the Union, with or without a cause. But secession is not revolution; it is ten thousand times worse; it is an anarchy. You do not wish to alter or abolish our form of government because it is an objectionable one. You are willing it should remain, but you wish to set up another government within our boundaries, and I am sure that if you do, you will model it after that to which you will have proved traitor, so well, in fact do you like it. Revolutionize the whole country if there is any cause for it."

"All governments derive their just powers from the consent of the governed, you know" said Bill.

"That is true, but Jefferson never meant that it was

necessary to have the consent of every one of the governed. The consent of the governed is the consent of the majority, and that the national government possesses. Twenty millions of people are devoted to their government."

"With some exceptions."

"While only a part of eight millions demand a change, and shall they rule the majority?"

"Let them rule themselves; it is all they ask."

"We will, but in a constitutional way. If every minority at the close of an election were allowed to secede, there would soon be nothing to secede from. Now if these malcontents were equally distributed over the whole country, they would be insignificant. Public opinion and the ballot-box would be sufficient remedies against their disorganizing tendencies. But the being all in a body together, in one section of the country, gives them an importance which their numbers do not deserve. Our government is one of their choice and adoption, and it is formed on the principle that the majority should rule. The majority ought to rule; there can be no free government without it."

"Why has not the South as good a right to secede from the United States, as the United Colonies had to secede from Great Britain in 1776?"

"Because her people have not the same cause. They offer none to the world. They have no decent respect to the opinions of mankind, and declare no cause for separation. Our fathers had numerous causes and they boldly declared them. They petitioned and remonstrated first, and the appeal to arms was the last resort. You southerners have nothing to say which you are not ashamed to embody in a declaration to the world, and there is a peaceful remedy for every just complaint that you can have."

"The question is who is to decide whether a people has cause to rebel. England did not think her American Colonies were right; you don't think the South is right. The rebels in 1776 thought differently, as they do now."

"The two cases are dissimilar. In one case there were real grievances; in the other there are none, and further, the colonies occupied a country which by their own toils and sufferings they had redeemed from the wilderness and its savage inhabitants—a country of their own, which was far removed from the ruling power in whose counsels they had no voice. They were on another continent. They did not set up a government in a corner of England. Even if the rule of England had been mild and just, it is impossible in the nature of things, and contrary to reason and natural justice that a country like this should long be subject to the sway of a little island across the ocean. But you would establish a nation within a nation. You have about the same right to secede that Yorkshire has. If the Southerners or the Yorkshiremen don't like their government, let them leave the country. They have no right to dictate to a majority what sort of government there shall be, or whether there shall be two governments or one."

"Revolutionists are always in a minority. If they were not they would not have to resort to revolution. The American colonies, taking the whole British Empire into consideration (and they were a part of it) were in a much greater minority than the Southerners are now in; and I don't see that a little water thrown between affects the question of right in the least."

"Water is a natural boundary of nations."

"Mountains are another, but you wouldn't see it, if the country west of the Rocky mountains was to rebel."

"No; we won't permit the establishment of any new government within the territory of the United States. Under a free government like ours, voluntarily accepted at first, there can be no cause for rebellion. If the people don't like their government, they have the power to alter it peaceably. The colonies did not have that power, nor any part of it.

"You talk well, but can you fight?" said Bill with a grim smile.

"That you will have a chance to prove if you go on."

"Success will make noble patriots of us rebels."

"If you wait for transformation, you will die dishonored traitors."

"Plainly, Tom, secession is the only salvation for slavery. If we remain it is doomed; if we go out we may preserve it. It is woven into the fabric of our society. We are born and bred in it and like it better than your system of so-called free labor, and think it the best condition of labor both for whites and blacks, so long as we have the negroes and cannot be rid of them. In fact all enforced labor, whether of poverty or the lash, is slavery. We find the institution of slavery to be both pleasant and profitable to us; many of your most prominent northern divines tell us it is scriptural and right, and we are bound to maintain it either within or without the Union."

After this manner their discussions usually proceeded and ended. Both were unconsciously pleased at the prospect of war, though they knew that when it came it would find them arrayed as enemies against each other. Darker and darker grew the threatening war-cloud which overhung the country. Sober patriots who knew how great a loss to them, their children and the world, would be the loss of the Union, grew grave and heavy-hearted at the prospect. Others thought there was needless alarm; that the sky would clear in a few months and that then we should go on again in our old way of peace and prosperity. No one fully anticipated the greatness of the impending conflict. But still the news from the South grew daily of a more warlike character. Daily did distinguished men previously honored for their ability and patriotism, fall away from the support of the government and throw themselves into the ranks of its enemies. The Union seemed to be dropping to pieces and fading away like some beautiful structure in a dream, to the surprise of those who knew that its stones were cemented with the blood of its builders, and expected it to stand. The Cabinet dissolved by resignation. Its rebel element withdrew after doing all the damage it could, to join the secession movement. Its loyal element, in the person of the venerable Cass, withdrew in disgust at the non-coercion policy of President Buchanan.

South Carolina seceded Dec. 20, 1860, and the announcement of the fact in the House of Representatives of the Congress of the United States was received with clapping of hands by a few secessionists. Major Anderson was fighting against starvation in Charleston harbor. The nation, like a headless trunk, remained passive under insults and injuries innumerable, raising no hand to defend its life against the blows of its would-be assassins.

New interest attached to the drill at the University and there was more hard study among the cadets of those branches of knowledge pertaining to war than the professors had witnessed for many a year.

Cadet Wolfe remained at the University, a hard student and outwardly loyal, until Georgia seceded, January 2, 1861. Then he transferred his allegiance from the national government to that of his native State and made his preparations to return home and take his position in the ranks of the gathering Southern chivalry.

He bade farewell to his companions, with less eloquence perhaps, but with more feeling, than Jefferson Davis exhibited in retiring from his place in the United States Senate, and wringing the hand of Tom Lyon while tears sprang to their meeting eyes, he departed for Washington, where his sister was at school, with the purpose of escorting her to their father's house.

On his arrival home he was received with a warm welcome, as were all the returning sons of the South, and very soon thereafter he received a captain's commission in a Georgia regiment and entered the service of the Confederacy.

CHAPTER IV.

THE STORM BURSTS—IT RAINS BLOOD—CADET LYON ENTERS HIS COUNTRY'S SERVICE—HONORS TO HIM AND PEACE BETWEEN NORWICH AND DARTMOUTH—OUR TWO HEROES AT SWORDS' POINTS.

DURING the remainder of Buchanan's term of office, the Union was a constant loser, while the South was gaining strength and material for the approaching conflict. Government property in the rebel states, forts, arsenals, navy-yards, ships, mints, custom-houses and sub-treasuries, with money, arms and munitions were taken, to the value of forty millions of dollars, without a single arm being raised in opposition.

A convention of the seceded states met at Montgomery, Alabama, and the Southern Confederacy was born there on the 9th of February, 1861.

When Lincoln came to take the reins of government he found himself at the head of a people paralyzed by the terrible state of affairs, despoiled of army, navy and war material, and without money or credit, while a formidable rebellion, fully organized and exultant at its first success, boldly confronted him and dared him to strike. Yet still he dreamed of peace, and in his inaugural address he attempted to pour oil upon the troubled waters which were rising to engulf the country and to blot from the galaxy of nations the brightest star which ever shone there. But his dream was quickly and rudely dispelled by the roar of a mortar from Sullivan's Island on the morning of the 12th of April. The news of the fall of Sumter flashed over the North, everywhere rousing the indignation of the people, who were stirred as they had never been before. It was quickly followed (April 15th) by the President's proclamation calling for 75,000 men, which was hailed with delight and responded to with alacrity. Vermont's first regiment was soon on its way to Washington under the command of Col. Phelps, the lamented Washburn being second in command.

The tide of secession which had flowed up to the very base of the Capitol began to ebb, and the cleansing waves from the hills of the North followed upon its returning course. Baltimore was humbled by Gen. Butler and made safe for the passage of loyal troops. Gen. McClellan "completely annihilated the enemy in Western Virginia." Gen. Butler took possession of Fortress Monroe and Newport News and forced the enemy to retire from Big Bethel to Yorktown, though at considerable loss to himself, owing to the blunders of his subordinates. Northern soldiers poured by thousands into Washington, and the armies of the West daily increased in numbers.

During these months of excitement cadet Tom Lyon remained at Norwich waiting for his graduation, which was to occur in July, but anxious to be engaged in the service of his country, and determined to be among the foremost to answer the next call upon Vermont for volunteers. He read with avidity all the news from the seat of war and rejoiced in every success of Northern arms. When news came from the disastrous field of Bull Run, casting a gloom over all the North and filling many hearts with dismay, Tom's cheek blanched a little, but it was with shame at the cowardice displayed, and not with fear of Southern valor.

He saw with secret joy that a ninety days' campaign was not to end the conflict as many had predicted.

"Now" said he to Condon, with a beaming face, "there will be another call and a chance for us."

"To feed the worms," added that hero. "You will enlist?" he inquired.

"Give your voice the falling inflection and you will be answered."

"To fall in a righteous cause is glorious, but very unpleasant, especially to a man of my proportions. I have made up my mind to enter upon the study of medicine so that I may be able to heal the wounds which you are likely to receive."

"I should rather face your sword than your scalpel, but there will be work for doctors before this war is over."

Mat did soon after enter a medical college, while Tom, receiving a Captain's commission, hastened with his regiment to join the army of the Potomac, then under the command of Gen. George B. McClellan, who had been called to supersede the venerable Scott.

Captain Lyon was at Norwich making a farewell visit among the undergraduates, when a telegram came, directing him to join his regiment at once. The cadets, with whom he was a general favorite, determined at once to escort him to the depot and accompany him as far as White River Junction, and for this purpose procured the use of two extra cars.

They marched out of town with music, but before they reached the descent overlooking the depot, the music ceased and they proceeded at "route step." As the first company came in sight of the depot they were surprised to see its platform and the adjacent grounds black with the students of Dartmouth.

A subdued murmur ran along the lines—"A fight! a fight! the Darties are out in force."

But just then from among the assembled students, who

were evidently waiting for the cadets, a clear voice rang out:—" Three cheers for Norwich University!"

These were given with hearty earnestness by the students.

The cadets were too much surprised to answer, even if it had been "military" to do so without orders. Never before in the history of the two institutions of learning, had a cheer for one emanated from the lungs of the students of the other.

The cadet in command ordered the direct step; the music sounded, and the companies marched down the hill to the station, wheeled into line and presented arms to Capt. Lyon, who gracefully raised his cap and withdrew.

Again the same voice heard before cried out—" Three cheers for Norwich University!"

Again the cheers resounded.

Then followed the quick commands—" Shoulder arms! order arms! in place, rest—Three cheers for Dartmouth College!"

These were given with all the strength of lung the cadets could muster.

Old Dartmouth had won this time. The cadets felt that they were fairly conquered by the magnanimity of their ancient foes.

When the train moved away from the depot a great number of students were on it and such friendly greetings as passed that day were never known before between cadets and students.

At White River Junction the train stopped and the large party assembled upon and about the platform of the depot. Cadet Carter, who had been selected by his fellow cadets for the duty, now advanced in their front and delivered a parting address to Capt. Lyon, which was distinguished for its good diction, noble sentiment and fervent patriotism and which was delivered in such an elegant and yet soldierly manner that the Dartmouth boys were somewhat astonished.

Our hero responded briefly but feelingly, and promised that he would never give his *alma mater* cause to be ashamed of him.

As he closed, the tall form of Staples appeared in the open space before the cadets, where he had been urged by his fellow students, and now being called upon for a speech, he said :—

"*Young Gentlemen of the Norwich University:*—At this crisis in our national affairs, when men of all parties are setting aside their differences to unite in the common defence of our country, it seems but proper that the students of Dartmouth and cadets of Norwich should settle their differences and unite also, if need be, in the service of the nation. In order to do this effectually, we owe you an apology, and I am selected to make it. Although we have never doubted your scholarship—your full equality with us in the arts and sciences—still we are obliged to confess that in the past we have looked upon you as a different class of young men from ourselves—a class of young men caught by the glitter and pomp of martial array, and we have thought that brass buttons and a neatly fitting uniform were the chief attractions of Norwich University in your eyes. We believed you were wasting your time in learning a science which could never be of service to you, while it curtailed your privileges and tied you down to irksome discipline. To day we see our mistake. You are not only fitted to compete with us in all the civil professions, but now, in this supreme hour of the nation's need, your military education makes you our superiors. You can buckle on the sword and *lead* men in the present conflict, while we of Dartmouth must shoulder the musket. For one, I declare that I should consider it an honor to serve under any graduate of Norwich University, and particularly under him to do honor to whom we are met to-day. (cheers.) I pledge you my word that before many months have passed away the armies of the republic shall be swelled by at least one raw recruit from Old Dartmouth, and on the muster-roll of his company you will find the name of Staples."

The speaker, as he concluded, was rapturously applauded. and then a general handshaking ensued.

The cadets and students returned together, and the former escorted the latter into Hanover. There they were received in the chapel and addressed by one of the professors, who referred in a happy manner to the unanimity of different parties, sects and cliques of men in view of the Union's peril.

A firm and lasting peace was thus established, and thereafter both parties regarded as their foes only the enemies of their common country.

By the middle of October, McClellan found himself at the head of 150,000 men, while his army was daily being increased by the arrival of regiment after regiment from the now determined North. Part of the troops were moved across the Potomac and encamped upon the "sacred soil" of Virginia, the regiment to which Capt. Lyon belonged among the rest.

The autumn and winter wore away in drilling the troops and preparing them for active service, while the country waited anxiously for a general advance. But the perhaps over-cautious commander-in-chief did not see fit to order one, and our soldiers did not enjoy the longed-for opportunity to measure their strength, on any important field. with the hosts of rebellion. Ball's Bluff and Drainesville relieved the monotony somewhat, but in neither of these engagements did our hero have a chance to distinguish himself. But while he fretted at inactivity, his first battle was not far distant.

Feb. 13th. Gen. Lander led 4000 men southward from the Potomac, and Tom's regiment was a part of this force.

They chose a route which would best screen them from the observation of the enemy's scouts, and reached the Great Cacapon at night. They spent half the night in throwing a rude bridge across this stream, but they worked not only with a will but with knowledge. Those Vermonters had worked out many a tax on the highways at home, and they knew something about bridge-building. They were veterans in the use of the ax, and the stringers were soon cut and fixed in their places. Where a party of cavaliers would have gazed hopelessly from bank to bank, or floundered in the water in attempting to cross, these sons of the roundheads went dry-shod, not through, but over the waters.

"Is this in your district?" said one brawny Green Mountain boy to another.

"Wal no; I guess not. We must be a leetle over the line, but, howsomever, I call my tax worked out."

The design of the commander was to surprise a force of the rebels at Blooming Gap, a short distance beyond, and the men were ordered to move as silently as possible.

Before day break they came within striking distance, and the scouts sent in advance reported the enemy unsuspicious of an attack.

The men were formed in proper order and the command given to advance. The enemy's pickets were driven in, alarming their friends as they retired. The rebels poured out of their tents half clad and half armed, and hastily, but imperfectly, formed to withstand the expected onset.

The Unionists with cheers charged upon the bewildered rebels.

"Follow me, Company A!" cried Captain Tom to his men, and sword in hand he led them, sweeping all before him.

It was a hand to hand fight among the rebel tents in the dim morning light, but the enemy was forced at every point to give way before the furious charge of our troops, who burned to wipe out the disgrace of Bull Run and to avenge the slaughter of their comrades at Ball's Bluff, where the gallant Baker yielded up as noble a life as the Union had to offer.

Many of the rebels fled in terror from the field, not to return. But others of a sterner courage were no sooner scattered in one quarter, then they re-formed in another, as though determined not to submit to defeat at the hands of the hated Yankees. Against these worthy foemen the Vermonters fought with a courage which would not have shamed their sires, and everywhere victoriously. Capt. Lyon's cold northern blood grew warm as though it flowed in southern veins, and his impetuosity and contempt of danger inspired his men with a confident courage that guaranteed success.

Not more than a fourth of the enemy now remained to dispute the field, and these were gathered together without much regard to military order. They were parts of different disorganized regiments and broken companies—a few of the bravest who stubbornly, but hopelessly, contended for victory.

A volley was poured into them which was returned with spirit and supplemented with yells of defiance.

The Vermonters, being in closest proximity to them, were ordered to charge, an order which they obeyed with alacrity.

"Come on, you cowardly hounds and pick out your graves; we'll dig them for you," came from the rebel ranks.

"We are coming, my friends," cried Tom, as his regiment rushed upon them.

The enemy withstood the shock and for a few minutes the combatants were intermingled. Swords and bayonets met and crossed in wild confusion.

Lyon's sword did not rest. No sooner had he cleared of foes a space around him, than he sprang again into the thickest of the fight. But his great strength and skill in the use of his weapon preserved him harmless.

Suddenly he found himself confronted by a young southern officer whose daring had several times turned the tide of battle momentarily in favor of the confederates.

Their swords crossed with a sharp ring, and then they looked each other in the face. It was light enough now to to distinguish countenances at such close quarters, and simultaneously there burst from their lips the familiar names—

"Bill!"

"Tom!"

The two friends were face to face on the field of battle. Instinctively they lowered their swords. Never before had they stood opposed. Before they could find further words, there was a rush made which separated them, and each found himself again in the midst of his own comrades. The momentary meeting seemed to both like a vision of the night.

Valor was of no avail to the rebels, surprised as they had been, and in a few minutes they were all put to flight, young Wolfe escaping with the rest. The contest had been as brief as it was fierce.

The Unionists took about a hundred prisoners in all, a comparatively large number of them being officers.

The dead, friend and foe, were buried, the spoils collected, the wounded cared for, and after a short interval for rest and refreshment, the expedition took up the line of march for camp, flushed with the triumph obtained, though it was decisive of nothing except the equal courage of northern and southern men.

Once more in the quiet of his tent, Capt. Lyon re-called his sudden and unexpected meeting with his old friend, and realized, more strongly than he had done before, the fraticidal nature of the strife in which he was engaged. He did not however feel any less inclination to prosecute it to a victorious issue. He felt that the integrity and perpetuity of the Union afforded to the world the brightest hope of universal freedom, and he determined to further, as much as in him lay, the accomplishment of the defiant prophecy of Andrew Jackson—" The Union must and shall preserved."

CHAPTER V.

BY THE CAMP FIRE—ON THE PENINSULA—WILLIAMSBURG—CAPT. LYON A PRISONER—AN UNEXPECTED MEETING.

FOR more than another month the main body of the army of the Potomac remained inactive. The younger officers tried to make the time pass as pleasantly as they could, and their endeavors were crowned with a fair measure of success. A few congenial spirits were in the habit of collecting together in Capt. Lyon's tent, and some of the evenings spent there were very enjoyable. The story, the song and jest went round as though no enemy were in the land, and war and bloodshed were things unknown. The party was usually made up of Capts. Lyon and Nason, Lieuts. Merritt and Safford, the latter's brother, Dr. Safford, and private Hank Wait. The last, inside the tent, was on an equality with his titled friends, who were all his former schoolmates and companions. They made no pretence of superiority, because there was none, except such as was made by their commissions and shoulder-straps. Our army was very democratic in character, especially the country regiments. Freemen, regarding all men as equal and accustomed to call no man lord, could not easily learn to look upon their officers as their superiors and respect them as such, when they had known them for years in civil life as no whit better than themselves—their social equals and co-laborers in peaceful pur suits. The officers themselves generally had the same feelings,—so different from the sentiment of the regular army, and from that to be observed in the standing armies of foreign countries.

But this feeling of equality between men and officers was not so conspicuous in city regiments, and is something which cannot endure through many campaigns in any regiment, though the rank and file be millionaires and Admirable Crichtons. An army is a perfect example of despotism. Though history proves that the citizens of republics —men accustomed to the enjoyment of liberty and equality —have generally made good and brave soldiers, it has been rather in spite of than because of the tyranny of army rule. Intelligent men who have volunteered to fight for a cause they esteem their own, determine to put up for a while with the necessary distinctions of rank, and to sacrifice, temporarily, their personal independence and equality for the common good. But none the less they know and feel—

"The rank is but the guinea's stamp,
The man's the gowd for a' that."

This democratic principle reigned supreme in Capt. Lyon's tent on the evenings when his friends met together for social enjoyment.

"I don't wear such handsome clothes as you fellows," Hank would frequently observe, "but I wear the handsomest face."

"Can't some one say something flattering about the Adonis-like form of our worthy private?" inquired Capt. Tom, pointing at the corpulent figure of Hank, who with an altitude of barely five feet five carried a weight of two hundred and thirty pounds avoirdupois.

"When I took lessons in drawing, in my youth, of the lady dauber at Green River Academy," said the tall and spare Dr. Safford, coiling his long legs two or three times around a camp-stool, "I was told that the curve is the line of beauty, and if that information was correct, I think that private Wait has numerous claims to beauty and those of no ordinary character."

"Perhaps you think the mullen the most graceful member of the vegetable kingdom," retorted Hank; "but if you do, you have as bad a taste as your physic."

"The Johnny rebs can't complain that Hank don't give hem a fair target," said Joe, who was known on parade as Lieut. Safford.

"I thought you was my friend, Joe," said Hank with an affected tone of injured feeling.

"I am, and I hope you'll remember that, and let me hide behind you in the day of battle."

"No need of that. There a'n't a sharp shooter on the other side able to hit such narrow strips of nothing as you and the Doctor."

"Come Merritt, sing us a song," cried Captain Nason. "These fellows are all so handsome and witty, that I begin to feel out of place in such fine company. We must do something brilliant or beat a retreat. Let me give you an overture to bring them to silence."

Seizing a violin, he gave it a few scrapes and turns of the keys, and then played with skill a lively tune which put his hearers in mind of festive scenes, where joy was unconfined.

Then in response to several invitations, Lieutenant Merritt sang in a clear, melodious voice the following song:

I sing of Vermonters, the bold and the free,
Whom foremost in battle their country shall see;
Who rush from their mountains like the spring torrent's flow,
And bathe the green vales with their blood as they go.
Like the fierce wind that blows through their tall mountain pines,
List the cheers in wild chorus that ring from their lines!
Undaunted by dangers, untrammeled by fears,
Beat the hearts in the breasts of Vermont's volunteers.

Afar thrown the scabbard when stirs the fierce strife,
They clutch the bright blade and each blow is a life;
With muscles of steel and with iron-like frame,
They write with their bayonets stories of fame.

Their springs of green hemlock—the badge of their State—
Wherever they wave are the gods' nod of fate.
O, the Green Mountain Boys, the bold mountaineers—
The pride of their State are Vermont's volunteers.

The arms that have wielded the scythe and the ax,
Can beat down the foe like the grass in their tracks;
And eyes that with rifle the wild hawk can take,
Can sight the broad mark that a traitor will make.
From boyhood to manhood, trained up in rough sports,
They know not the polish of courtiers and courts,
But where there are deeds that befit men to do,
There, foremost, Vermonters stand gallant and true.
Their bayonets gleam on the fair Southern plain,
Whose blossoms are painted with blood of the slain,
And grimly the mountaineer leans on his gun,
On the field of fierce carnage his valor has won.

But the thoughts of his home, of his dear mountain home,
Where the green hemlocks bend to the breezes that roam—
These start down the powder-grimed cheek the warm tears
Which flow from the hearts of Vermont's volunteers.

Where the loved ones were left in the snug little cot,
'Mid the charms of a home which can ne'er be forgot;
Where the rich yellow grain upon upland and vale,
'Neath the bluest of skies, grows ripe for the flail.
There the soldier will gaze through the mist of his tears,
But to gather new courage and kill coward fears.
Hurrah! for Vermont! for her bold mountaineers!
Hurrah! for Vermont! and Vermont's volunteers!

The singer ceased, and there was silence for a few moments, for in every mind tender thoughts of home had been aroused and contended with patriotic emotion for the mastery. The Doctor, who was the only married man in the company, had an absent look upon his face.

"Bravo! Lieutenant," cried Capt. Nason. "I think we may venture to stop here a while longer. If our courage and patriotism need the spur, you have given it to us."

"We must fight! I repeat it gentlemen, we must fight!" exclaimed Hank.

"Let us smoke first," suggested Joe, "you will have a chance to lard the lean earth, yet, Falstaff, in some future Bull Run."

"Fill your pipes gentlemen—pure Virginia, I assure you—and then I shall call for a story from Dr. Safford," said Tom.

"Let me speak a piece," said Hank.

"Peace, peace; there is no peace," and we don't wish any from you. A story from the Doctor."

"Shoulder your crutch—"

"And saddle-bags—"

"And tell how fields are won."

"No doubt you need to know," replied the Doctor, "but I don't wish to usurp the prerogative of the commander-in-chief. If I must tell a tale, it will have to be one of the future—and such an one as I shall tell my grandchildren."

"Have it as as you please, and begin."

"Give us the title and say—Chapter I., but remember we don't want any continued story."

"My story is called

"THE PATHWAY TO GREATNESS."

"Years ago, my dear grandchildren, when I was young, and your mother was a baby, occurred the great rebellion of which you have read in your school histories. There was a young man whom I knew well, named Thomas Lyon, and he was as full of courage as the animal whose name he bore. He went to the war as a captain. He would have gone as a private, but the government would not permit it. He had a genius for command and it was thought best to clothe him with authority. In his first battle he became frenzied with excitement and rushed alone and singlehanded upon the enemy, though he knew not, at the time, whither he was rushing. His men, inspired by his example, charged recklessly after him, and the victory was won. For this exhibition of gallant conduct, he was made a colonel. In his next battle he was surprised with his regiment between two detatchments of the enemy, each of which poured in a galling fire upon his melting ranks. It was death to remain there and it seemed certain destruction to move in either direction. But his men got tired of being shot down like sheep in a pen, and charged desperately upon that portion of the enemy which had got between them and the main body of the Union army. It was a charge home, and nothing could withstand it. What they did not kill of the enemy, they drove into their own camp as prisoners. In his report of the battle, the commanding general described the affair as a dashing and successful attempt to divide and thus conquer the force of the enemy. The colonel was immediately promoted to the rank of brigadier general.

In the following campaign, a certain Gen. Ryan was severely wounded in a desperate assault upon rebel earthworks. In the report of this, a mistake was made, owing to the similarity of names, and Gen. Lyon was declared the hero. By this lucky accident, my friend became a major general. Not being engaged in any other battles, he served creditably through the remainder of the war, and, at its close, retired upon his laurels and the money he had saved out of his salary. In the years of peace which followed, he devoted himself to politics with the same success which he enjoyed in war, ever moving onward in the pathway to greatness. He filled successively the highest offices in the gift of his native state, and finally a grateful people, as represented by the Old Soldiers' Party, nominated him for the Presidency. He was triumphantly elected and re-elected, serving two terms. Declining a third election, his statue was placed in the Capitol, which it at present adorns. And thus you see, my dear grandchildren, I shall remark, "how the humblest merit may rise to the loftiest position." And my grandson Philip will proudly exclaim, "Grandpa knew that man! How I wish there would be another war."

"Well, Doctor," said Tom, after allowing the others to laugh, "I don't want another story, and if I did, I don't think I should call on you for it."

After much further converse upon different topics, Captain Lyon's guests departed for their respective tents, and soon silence settled down upon the great army sleeping upon the hostile soil of the Old Dominion. Camp-life was made comparatively pleasant by those who were determined to be happy, as almost any kind of life can be made, but the most careless knew that there was stern work to be done and hardships to be endured before their flag could wave again over a united country.

Early in March, the enemy abandoned its winter camp and retired southward, and soon after there was an advance of our grand army upon Centreville and Manassas which were found deserted. Having held, occupied and possessed these positions without bloodshed, our anaconda army turned its head toward the Potomac again, while with its tail it drove Stonewall Jackson up the Shenandoah Valley.

During the latter part of the month, the main body of the army was transferred to Fortress Monroe, where Gen. McClellan arrived on the 2d of April and the Peninsula Campaign began. Our army was over 100,000 strong and opposed at first only by the rebel Gen. Magruder, who held Yorktown with about 8,000 men. Had the true state of affairs then been known, a determined advance might have forced the Confederacy into its last ditch and saved us the blood and treasure of the sword-fish policy of Gen. Grant, which was afterward found necessary. But this would have spoiled our story, as well as the reputation of sundry heroes who won fame for themselves in the succeeding campaigns.

For thirty days the army was employed in throwing up earth-works for the siege of Yorktown. When about ready to drive Magruder from his works, he saved them the trouble and expense of powder by quietly withdrawing and retreating up the peninsula.

The pursuit was begun by Stoneman's cavalry, which was followed by Hooker's, Kearney's and three other divisions towards Williamsburg, where the enemy was strongly entrenched. This first battle for the possession of Richmond was mainly fought by Hooker's division, and resulted in a victory to our arms, though at a total loss of over 2,000 men.

The forest was felled for a breadth of half a mile in front of the rebel works, to obstruct the advance of our troops. Two regiments were sent into the timber, while the others, with two batteries, advanced into the cleared field on the right.

Now, for the first time, Capt. Lyon found himself engaged in a great battle, and he and his fun-loving companions of the Potomac camp proved that they could fight as well as laugh and sing.

"Now Tom," said Nason, as he came near, "is a chance to fulfill the doctor's prophecy and win a colonel's commission."

"I don't think I'm crazy enough yet for that, but where is he?—in the rear waiting to saw off our legs?"

"I'm here, Thomas," said the tall surgeon just behind him; "I want to be on hand when you run against one of those 'bare bodkins' over yonder."

"Thank you," replied Lyon, as Fort Magruder again opened upon them, dropping all conversation in the roar of its guns.

Soon after a large body of Confederates were seen charging towards them in gallant style, yelling as they came.

"Steady, boys, steady," sounded along the line; "don't fire till you are ordered."

"And then don't waste your powder—fire low," said Lt. Joe to his men.

On came the enemy with furious speed. It required great courage calmly to wait their approach.

"Stand firm!" growled Lyon to his company.

"You can count on me; I am too fat to run," replied Hank, raising a laugh even in that moment of peril.

The enemy were within a few rods of them—their faces plainly distinguishable.

"Fire!" rang out in a clear tone.

A tremendous volley was poured into the advancing foe, nearly every bullet doing execution.

The rebels fell by scores; their ranks were broken; they halted and staggered as though uncertain whether to advance or retreat.

"Fire!" rang out again the same clear voice.

Another volley, fired with equal effect, completed the demoralization of the enemy. They turned and fled.

"Upon them, boys!" cried Capt. Lyon, waving his sword and dashing forward followed by his men.

"I can't run, but I will walk," said Hank, and he followed slowly after, loading as he went.

Pursuit was useless, as well as dangerous, owing to the nearness of the rebel batteries, and Company A, with its impetuous Captain, was quickly re-called by the commanding officer.

Twice more the rebels charged the position held by the Green Mountain Boys, each time with fresh troops and with increased numbers and more resolute purpose. But each time they were repulsed with great slaughter, though not without inflicting severe loss upon their opponents. Here sank down many to mingle their ashes with the dust of an empire built upon slavery—voiceless but perpetual pleaders for that liberty for which they died—and the friends they left in northern homes looked with unsatisfied eyes to see their faces among the returning brave.

Gen. Longstreet's division of the rebel army now arrived on the field, and a fresh attempt was made to push back our forces. The struggle was long and of doubtful issue, but the enemy was at last repulsed, though our soldiers used up all their ammunition and all they could find in the boxes of their dead comrades, before they accomplished the repulse of their determined assailants.

But the desperate courage displayed could not alone, in every case, command success. Another assault on our front from the direction of Fort Magruder found our men with only bayonets to repel it.

As the enemy came on, once more the order was given to charge and meet them. With a northern cheer, which equalled in volume the southern yell, our men sprang forward. Hand to hand they fought till the dead and dying lay thick upon the ground, which was red with their blood. Capt. Lyon displayed a valor which brought upon him the particular attention of the enemy.

"Stand to them!" he cried; "not a step backward!" as his sword flashed in the air and descended with a force which sent his nearest antagonist a corpse to the earth. Again it flashed, reeking with blood and fell with a death-blow. But the odds were too great in the advanced position he was attempting to hold. His foes swarmed about him; they made a rush which forced back our troops, and when the rebel wave retired, it carried with it about two hundred of our men as prisoners. Among them was Capt. Lyon, disarmed and furious at his capture, but, thanks to his good sword and his good training, without a single wound.

"Come, Yank; you're bagged. Double-quick it now —we can't stop here," said one of his captors, hurrying him along.

"You want to go to Richmond so bad it would be a pity to prevent you," said another.

"I reckon if he can't take Richmond, that Richmond can take him," said a third jocose rebel.

Tom deigned no reply to these remarks, but hoping yet to be recaptured before the close of the battle, he was taken within the rebel lines and sent to the rear.

His hopes of recapture were not destined to be fulfilled. That night the Confederates evacuated Williamsburg, leaving the disputed field to be occupied by our army. In this particular the battle was a victory to our arms, but our loss, over 2,000 in killed, wounded and prisoners, was probably quite as large as that of the enemy. We took over a thousand prisoners, a larger number than we lost, but the most of them were wounded men whom the enemy abandoned in their hasty retreat.

Gen. McClellan claimed the victory in the following dispatch to the Secretary of War:

"HEADQUARTERS ARMY OF THE POTOMAC,
Williamsburg, May 6, 1862.

Hon. E. M. Stanton, Secretary of War:—Every hour proves our victory more complete. The enemy's loss is great, especially in officers. I have just heard of five more of their guns captured. Prisoners are constantly arriving.

G. B. McCLELLAN,
Maj.-Gen. Commanding."

The night after the battle, our hero found himself on the road to Richmond, against his will. He did not know how the battle had gone, but rightly judged by the evidences of retreat around him, that it had gone in favor of the Union. He bitterly regretted the prospect of inactivity before him while he marched along with his fellow-prisoners, guarded by rebels on every side. Among them were a few prisoners from a New Hampshire regiment and as Tom scanned their faces, he thought he recognized one who wore a captain's uniform. At the same time the New Hampshire man, probably also looking for a familiar face, glanced at our hero, and with a peculiar smile approached him and extended his hand.

It was Sophomore Staples of Dartmouth College, cadet Wolfe's antagonist in the battle of Hanover, described in a former chapter.

"Friends, now, Captain, are we?" inquired Staples.

"Yes," returned Tom frankly, grasping the extended hand, "friends and brothers in misfortune."

"*Felicitas multos habet amicos*—prosperity has many friends—adversity but few," said the collegian.

"True," returned Tom; "and those of prosperity not only fall away from us, but often become our enemies," sadly thinking, as he spoke, of his friend Bill.

"That reminds me," said the other, "of my former enemy and victor. What has become of him?"

"He is in the confederate service, and probably with this army."

"I hope he won't feel it due to his honor to finish the job of killing me which he began so vigorously on that night, you remember," said Staples, laughing.

"Never fear; Wolfe is as noble as he is brave. He never attacks any one unless he feels pretty sure that the chances are in favor of his being whipped in the encounter. I don't think he will ever distinguish himself in the pursuit of a beaten enemy."

Thus conversing together, the two walked on cheerfully to prison.

That same evening the friends of Capt. Lyon, missing him, sought his body on the field of battle; but no trace of him was found.

"Not dead, then, it is certain," said Capt. Nason.

"Probably wounded and taken prisoner" said Lieutenant Merritt.

"Our future president is no doubt a prisoner," said Dr. Safford, deliberately, "but it is my opinion that he is not seriously wounded, if at all. We know that the rebels have left their own wounded behind them, and it is not likely that they have taken any of ours."

In this opinion all coincided, and somewhat relieved, yet sad at the loss of the favorite of the mess, they returned to the bivouac of the regiment and cast themselves down upon the ground to sleep as well as they could amid such horrible surroundings—all except the Doctor, who was busy all night, nearly, in attending to the wounded.

CHAPTER VI.

LIBBY PRISON—COL. WOLFE—HELOISE—CÆSAR, ONE OF THE BONES OF CONTENTION—LOVE—A HOPE OF ESCAPE.

APTAINS Lyon and Staples were conducted to Richmond and lodged in Libby prison, where they were treated with as much kindness as they had reason to expect. They had nothing to complain of except that they were prevented from participating in the fighting which they knew to be going on around the rebel capital in which they were confined.

Their anxious inquiries elicited no satisfactory responses from the jailor, but they rested in the confident hope that McClellan would prove victorious, and, making a triumphal entry into Richmond, burst open the doors of their prison and set them free.

Had they known the actual result of the Seven Days' battle—that the star-spangled banner was being trailed in the mire of retreat through White Oak Swamp, instead of waving aloft in advance on Richmond—they would have hummed the national anthem a few times less than they did. But they could not long remain in ignorance of the truth. The air was full of tidings from the battlefield, and the very wind seemed to tell of success to the Confederate arms.

Portions of the victorious rebel army entered the city, and the shoutings and rejoicings sufficiently corroborated the story of the wind.

The two prisoners grew melancholy, but more at the defeat of their comrades than at their own unpleasant condition.

"The prospect isn't very cheering," remarked Lyon.

"No," returned Staples. "I fear a great disaster has befallen our army; perhaps it has been destroyed."

"I don't believe that such an army as we had has allowed itself to be destroyed or captured. It has been forced to retire, no doubt, but there is fight left in it yet, and these jubilant individuals, outside our present residence, will find it out some future day."

The door swung open and a Confederate colonel entered the room. With a hasty glance at the inmates, he stepped quickly towards Captain Lyon. The Norwich Cadets confronted each other.

The two friends clasped hands. Smiles lighted up their faces, while there was a suspicious moisture in their eyes. The circumstances in which they again met impressed them with some feelings of sadness, but they were soon cast off. Shaking his friend's hand heartily, Bill exclaimed in the merry voice of old:

"Welcome to Richmond!"

"Thank you," returned Tom, in the same tone, "for your cordial hospitality; and allow me to express the hope that, at no distant day, I may have the pleasure of welcoming you to the land of the free and the home of the brave."

"I shall be happy to see you at any time, I assure you, but I prefer that the meeting be on some other soil. I fear, as our friend Condon could poetically express it—

"'The land of the free
Would prove a prison to me.'"

Bill here glanced at Capt. Staples inquiringly. The latter approached as if doubtful of the reception he would meet with.

"Allow me, Col. Wolfe," said Tom, "to bring to your remembrance an old acquaintance—Capt. Staples of Hanover, formerly commander of the Dartmouth Sophomore Brigade."

"A second time your vanquished enemy," said Staples.

Bill took his hand while he laughingly replied—

"I ask a truce to bury old animosities. I see that Tom is now on your side, and I fear he would not step in to save me from a whipping, as he did when we met before."

Friendly relations being thus established, the three sat down for a pleasant conference upon things past and present. Each had many inquiries to make, and much information to impart, and the time passed so agreeably that the two Unionists almost forgot that they were prisoners, and that their pleasant companion wore the uniform of an enemy.

"Promotion must be rapid in the Confederate service," said Tom, pointing to his friend's shoulder straps.

"It has to be, that we may keep up with you. We don't commence as brigadiers," returned Bill.

"How happened you to find us out so soon?" inquired Tom, "I feared I should not see you."

"I heard some Yankee officers were taken, and knowing your natural tendency to get into trouble, I thought you might be one of them, and came to see."

"I am very glad you came, and hope you will excuse me if I don't return your call. Circumstances beyond my control oblige me to keep the house quite closely for the present."

"You are quite excusable."

"Tell me," continued Tom, "if there is anything left of our army,—if it won't be giving too much information to the enemy. I suppose we have been whipped."

"I think you have been—sorry to pain you with disagreeable news—and your whole army *has* left, not *is* left, though most of it is safe enough for the present. Little Mac. has 'changed his base,' I think he calls it that."

After some further talk, Col. Wolfe rose to take his leave.

"Keep up your spirits boys; it is the fortune of war that we should be vanquished sometimes; we can't always be victors. I will call on you as often as I can until my regiment moves, and, meanwhile, I will see that your rations are improved in quality, and that you are supplied with tobacco."

"Go, miserable comforter, but don't forget the tobacco," replied Tom, as the door closed behind his friend.

This visit was as a gleam of sunshine within the walls of Libby, and the prisoners felt more reconciled to their confinement for knowing that they had at least one personal friend among the enemy.

The next morning they found their breakfast superior to anything which they had experienced before, and they were able to supplement it with some fine cigars, a box of which had been handed them by the jailor.

In the afternoon they received another visit from Col. Wolfe. He entered, accompanied by a young lady whom he introduced as his sister.

Heloise Wolfe was about eighteen years of age, of slight but graceful form, clear brunette complexion and fine regular features. Her eyes were large, black and eloquent and her wavy hair, of the same hue, was of luxuriant growth. She had a bright sparkling beauty calculated to dazzle the beholder, but beauty was not her only charm. Possessed of superior intelligence without being strong minded, in the late sense of that abused term; animated in conversation, without being disposed to monopolize it; of high principle and earnest nature; generous, impulsive and sincere, with a dash of the chivalric temperament of her brother, whom she strongly resembled, she was a sister to be proud of, as Col. Wolfe evidently thought. Capt. Lyon, as he gazed upon her with poorly concealed admiration, felt like transferring his affection from the brother to the sister.

"My sister has heard so much of you, Capt. Lyon—of your prowess, beauty, etc.,—that on hearing you had taken up your residence temporarily among us, and that I was coming to see you, she insisted on accompanying me,—doubting I suppose, whether she would otherwise have an opportunity of making your acquaintance. I tried to dissuade her by telling her you were one of the vandal army come to sack our cities and desolate our homes, and that it was a part of her duty, as a southerner, to hate all such. She, however, thought it only a Christian duty to visit the prisoner, and I finally allowed her to come."

"You know my brother Willie so well, Capt. Lyon," said Miss Heloise, smiling in so distracting a manner that the Union officer felt himself doubly a prisoner, "that you will interpret his speech correctly. It means that I feel it not only a duty, but a pleasure to visit one whom my brother esteems so highly as he does yourself."

"I am sure your motives are worthy of you, Miss Wolfe, and I thank you for the honor you do me, but I fear your brother has spoken more highly of me than I deserve," replied Capt. Lyon, bowing low before the young lady.

"My gallant friend exemplifies the saying that true merit is always modest," said Col. Wolfe.

"True friendship ought not to be so satirical," said Lyon. "Be merciful."

"I doubt whether I ought to show much mercy to an enemy of the Confederacy. It would be setting a bad example."

"My brother is suspicious of my loyalty," said Heloise, "because I cannot get over my love for the old flag."

"Thank God you cannot," replied Lyon warmly, growing more enamored of her as he perceived that she was not a venomous secessionist.

"Treason! cried Bill, half in earnest, half in jest.

"That can be no crime in the Confederacy," said Tom. "The divine right of treason is the very soul of your government."

"So I tell them," said Heloise, gleefully, and that I have a right to secede all alone by myself if I choose."

"I think I had better take you away, Miss, before you are utterly perverted. The very air is tainted with unionism here," said her brother.

"You see, Captain, my reputation for southern loyalty is not very good."

"I trust your charitable kindness in visiting a Union prisoner will not give you an unpleasant reputation in your circle of friends. If it does I shall regret the visit, much as it has brightened one day of a tiresome captivity."

"Never fear for her, Tom," said Bill; "no one has thought of indicting her for treason yet."

"No; they let me say what I please, because, I suppose, they think I'm not worth minding."

Tom did not say, but he looked as if he was of the opinion that they were very stupid who thought so.

"It is really time that we should go," said Bill, suddenly growing serious, as he took his friend's hand. "I have left my bad news unsaid till the last. My regiment leaves to-morrow; Tom and I cannot tell when we shall meet again. I have taken measures to have you made comfortable as long as you remain here, and my sister will further my intentions as much as she is able."

"Your generosity is appreciated, Bill, but I would be content on half rations if they were seasoned with your company. But you must go, of course. I can't wish you success—my patriotism won't admit of that—but I do hope you will be taken prisoner and kept in close confinement till the close of the war."

"Thank you for your good wishes, Tom, but I hope they are not prophetic."

Good-bye was said, and Wolf and his sister retired.

"A glorious fellow!" exclaimed Staples, who very much admired his former antagonist.

"*She is*" returned Capt. Lyon, abstractedly, gazing at a patch of sky through the grated window.

Our hero did not appear to be very communicative during the remainder of the day and evening, and Staples finally gave up the attempt to engage him in conversation. He was busy with his own thoughts, but whether they were sad or pleasant was not discernible. The next day, however, he was more companionable; but now that Col. Wolfe came no more to visit them our friends would have found their life at Libby almost intolerable had not Miss Heloise taken it upon herself to show a generous kindness to her brother's friend.

Her father held office under the confederate government and the family, therefore, resided at Richmond. The doors of Libby prison were open to Heloise, without question, whenever she chose to enter them and she frequently visited the Yankee prisoners accompanied by her sable attendant, Cæsar, a young slave about twenty years old, born and bred in the family and entirely devoted to his handsome young mistress.

Cæsar was a well built young fellow, as black as ebony, with teeth and eyes in remarkable contrast with his shining skin. Of a happy and faithful disposition and possessed of much natural shrewdness, he was a favorite family servant and occupied a much easier position in life than human chattels generally do.

"How happens it," said Capt. Lyon one day to Cæsar, "that with such a name as yours, you are not in the army?"

"Didn't pick out my own name, massa; dunno noffin' 'bout war; young massa William do all de fightin' for de family. I'se willin'; de smell ob powder am stremely obnoxious to dis child."

Heloise brought books and papers which helped greatly to relieve the monotony of prison-life, and many delicacies, which were not in the prison bill of fare, found their way to the room occupied by our friends. But more highly prized than the material comforts which she brought, was the pleasure of her company. She generally sat down and spent some time in cheerful conversation, and the moments thus brightened seemed to shed a radiance over all the remaining day.

In the interchange of sentiment which occurred on these occasions, which were quite frequent, the acquaintance of Capt. Lyon with his friend's sister gradually ripened into a tender intimacy.

As this fact became apparent to the sharp eyes of Capt. Staples, he withdrew himself as much as possible from the company of the lovers, offering as a poor apology, when his silence was noticed—which was not often—his absorbing interest in the book he was reading. On one such occasion he had a volume of sermons and having read one of these, without looking at the title, he was exercising his ingenuity in guessing at the text. With all his Yankee talent in that direction, however, he was very wide of the mark.

Our hero found that Heloise was at heart a Union woman; that she very much regretted the disruption of those ties which bound the North and South together and contributed so much to their strength, prosperity and happiness, and that she was far from feeling satisfied with the position which her father and brother had seen fit to take.

H

She cordially sympathized with Lyon in his aspirations after a restoration of the Union and grieved over disaster to the federal arms which threatened, at the least, to delay the day of triumph. She did not forget that the gallant man in whom she felt a growing interest owed to his patriotism, his deprivation of liberty, and she tried to console him as best she could, in his irksome confinement, and to reconcile him to the inactivity which seemed decreed.

"When first taken prisoner," said he, "I felt that I could hardly endure a protracted confinement, and know that while I was unable to strike a blow, my brave companions would be fighting the battles of our country."

"I know you long to be with your regiment again, devastating, as Will says, the fair homes of the South, but you must try to be patient."

"I think that of late I am learning to excel in that virtue. Since captivity led me to you, Heloise, I feel like blessing the fate that made me captive."

"And yet, how your eyes would brighten to learn that you were to be exchanged."

"I fear that they would weep. Is treason infecting my heart, or "———

"Love," said Staples, reading unconsciously aloud, "is the fulfilling of the law."

The speakers glanced hurriedly at the reader, but he seemed not to be aware of their presence, and ignorant of having taken any part in the conversation.

"My friend is no doubt correct," said Tom, smiling and speaking in a lower tone, "but Uncle Sam has other views of a soldier's duty."

"Not if the love be love of country," said Heloise intently regarding the floor, "that is the grander passion."

"Ah! I know, I love my country, Heloise, but that is not the love that reconciles me to captivity."

"No; nor does any other. You would break through these barred windows, if you thought that liberty was on the outside of them."

Lyon half rose from his seat, as if a new idea had struck him, then sinking back, said slowly, " 'Tis true: I should: but I should love you none the less."

"You confess you would desert me, if you could," said Heloise, playfully.

"Not you, but Richmond."

In a little while, Heloise with Cæsar took her departure, Staples rising long enough to bid her good afternoon.

But when the door was closed, locked and bolted, and the prisoners were left alone again, the New Hampshire man sat down with a yawn over the shut book of sermons, which he held in his hand, and then, turning his eyes sleepily toward the beaming face of his companion, he inquired—

"Lyon, have you been reading this sermon on the "Cheerful uses of Adversity?'"

"No, why do you ask?"

"Because you seem to be growing happier every day, and I am sure we are in adversity."

"We are in the hands of our adversaries, but why let them restrain our spirits as well as our bodies?"

"I can't guess: I give it up."

"You are getting low-spirited."

"Perhaps; I don't think I am getting high spirited."

"Don't give up to despair yet: there are brighter days in store for us."

"Glory waits us you think: but won't it get tired waiting?"

"No: I feel a wonderful elation and hopefulness."

"Much greater than when we first entered these walls, do you not?"

"Yes; I do."

"I understand it, Lyon, and I congratulate you. I experience, indeed, by sympathy, a small share of your happiness, but it does not suffice me."

"What are you firing at, comrade?"

"Not at your happiness, tantalizing as it is. You presented a much more consoling spectacle when you were as miserable as myself."

"I shall have to flog you Staples, if you don't stop talking with such oracular mistiness. Out with it: what are you trying to say?"

"We grow hard-hearted as fortune smiles upon us," returned Staples, smiling at his friend's threat.

"Well, I'm listening," said Tom.

"I do not envy your happiness, I hope; certainly I do not wonder at it, and you ought not to wonder at my misery."

"I thought happiness contagious. Why are you not happy when you think that I am?"

"Because I can't make love to Cæsar."

"Well," said Tom, laughing, "I plead guilty to want of consideration for your desolate condition, and I will wear as unhappy a countenance as I can assume hereafter."

"Then we will be fraternally and happily miserable together."

"Yes, so long as we are forced to remain here; but listen Staples," said Lyon lowering his voice, "it has occurred to me to-day, for the first time, that we have not shown much spirit in staying cooped up here so long without making an effort to regain our liberty."

"Perhaps not; but do you imagine that we could take Richmond, if we could get out of here?"

"No: but I imagine it might give Richmond some trouble to re-take us."

"I should hope so; too much trouble to make it worth while; for if we were taken we should not, probably, get such comfortable quarters as these, nor should we be likely to see again the smiling countenance of Cæsar."

"We run of course the risk of getting severer treatment, if we fail."

"But can we break out of this?" said Staples with some eagerness.

"I think we can, though I have not yet contrived the method. We must consider the obstacles in the way of our escape and the means of overcoming them."

"We are on the second floor," said Staples, looking out of the window, "and if we could get through here, might jump."

"That won't do; it is paved below. We should break our legs and that would be the end of it. We can manufacture a rope easily enough out of our clothing and slide down without danger."

"So far, well! how shall we get through the window? And if we get through and reach the ground safely, how shall we escape the watchman? And if we escape him, how shall we get out of the city, guarded as it is by policemen and soldiers, and we utter strangers to it and dressed in federal uniform? And if we get out, how shall we find our way through this hostile country and find provision till we reach the free soil?"

"You have said enough to dampen any one's ardor a little," returned Lyon. "but still I have a hope that we may succeed. It is well to look these difficulties all in the face and be ready to meet them. We will take time to mature our plan and leave as little to good luck as possible. There is no use in taking the first step, unless there is a reasonable prospect of being able to take the second and the third and fourth also."

"Let us sleep on it; I am always wisest in my dreams."

"One of us may have a vision of a safe path to freedom, so good night."

They lay down to rest but it was long before either fell asleep, their minds were so full of the subject of conversation. And when at last they slept, their minds worked on. They dreamed, but we will leave their dreams to another chapter.

CHAPTER VII.

DREAMS OF LIBERTY—PLANS FOR ESCAPE—A NIGHT WATCH—FAREWELL TO HELOISE.

"GOOD morning," exclaimed Staples, as his eyelids flew open like the lids of a spring watch case, at the first touch of the rosy fingers of Aurora.

"Good morning," returned his companion drowsily. "Tell me your dream while I'm waking up."

"No, begin you."

"As you please, but nothing in my dream will prove of any practical importance. Not a hint was given me in regard to the ways and means of escape. I dreamed that I was again among my friends and with our army, encamped somewhere on the Potomac, in the neighborhood of Washington, but how I got there I have not the faintest remembrance."

"Not much of a dreamer, you. The conditions were highly favorable, and yet you made nothing of them. Now listen to me," said Staples, giving the finishing pull at his necktie. "I dreamed that the Goddess of Liberty, who bore a striking resemblance to Miss Wolfe, threw open our door and beckoned to me to follow her. With the courage of Hamlet, I obeyed and followed where she led, through the door down the stairs and out into the open air. It was night; the guard slept; the city was silent; the sky was clear and the moon so bright that the street-lamps performed a useless office. I saw standing near the prison wall a close carriage of diminutive size, but elegant shape and delicate workmanship. It was of burnished gold with silver wheels. Harnessed to it—the buckles of their harnesses thickly studded with glistening diamonds—were four cream colored horses with flowing white manes and tails and with wings upon their feet. They beat the air impatiently with their feet, but did not move the vehicle to which they were attached. The Goddess motioned me to enter. Observing that Cæsar was on the box, I sprang in without question and closed the door after me. While I was observing the gorgeous and luxurious furnishing of the inside, I heard the whip crack and immediately perceived that we were in rapid motion, although no sound was audible save that of swiftly beating wings. Instead of dashing along the street, as I had expected, we rose at once into the air with great velocity. Higher and higher we ascended, until, looking from the window, I saw the spires of Richmond far below. Then we turned our course northward and flew with the speed of the wind over the roadway of cloud, the wheels flashing as though they were wheels of light. There was no stop or turn. Nothing impeded our progress or slackened the speed of our tireless steeds. Though conscious of my lofty altitude, I had a feeling of greater security than I generally have when driving along country highways, and it seemed to me the most easy and pleasant method of travelling that I ever experienced. At the gait we went, however, our journey necessarily soon came to an end. As we drew near Washington, we began to descend, making an angle with our former course of about thirty degrees, and finally touched the earth in front of the Capitol. This means that I shall be a congressman sometime. As I was about to alight, there was a burst of flame around me, in which my whole establishment, horses, carriage, Cæsar and all, vanished in an instant, and I woke up to find the sun shining brightly in my eyes through the barred window of our prison."

"Staples, I would never wake up again," if I were you. Your sleeping fancy is to your waking, as feathers to lead," said Tom, when the other had finished his narration. "I suppose the interpretation of your dream is that you will escape and I shall not, as I was not invited to take passage with you in that handsome Concord buggy, which the New Hampshire men always dream of, when they dream of going anywhere."

"You are as bad at interpreting dreams as you are at dreaming. According to the proper interpretation of the dream, it is very clear to me that if either of us is to be left behind, that one will be myself."

"By the same rule I am to be congressman, also."

"An intelligent people must decide between us."

"Well, we won't dispute now about so very distant an honor. Explain your dream in your own way. What do you find in it that we can turn to our account?"

"My dream, to me, is encouraging. It gives me an idea which would not otherwise have occurred to me. You will remember that my goddess resembled Miss Wolfe. She is, for us, the Goddess of Liberty. She can, and will, I think, if we confide in and appeal to her, assist us to escape from this prison and the city. Once free, outside the limits, we will strike across the country (I wish we could go through the air) towards Washington. With a few tools, which she could easily bring us, we could soon let ourselves out of this building, and then with a carriage and disguises which she could furnish, we could make our way out of the city. That is what my dream tells me."

"It could be done in the way you say, I have no

I

doubt; but, in your eagerness to escape, you forgot one thing, and that is, that the plan you propose is unworthy of us and therefore not to be adopted. Miss Wolfe is loyal to the Union and would not hesitate to assist us, I feel sure, if we were to divulge our plan to her, but we cannot abuse her generous sympathy. Since she is the person who visits us and the only one in the city with whom we are acquainted, she could not render us the assistance you speak of, without subjecting herself to the risk of almost certain discovery."

"You are right Lyon, we cannot ask her to compromise herself for us in such a way. I beg you to believe I do not seek my liberty at her expense. I must dream again."

"Perhaps a little thinking, with our eyes open, would do as well. Let us look over this place and see what we have to do."

An examination of the windows showed that it would be necessary to remove at least two of the iron bars, which crossed the lower part of each window, in order to admit the passage of a man's body. To do this work, they had only two stout pocket knives, but these they thought would enable them to loosen one end of each of the two bars and then, with their united strength, they could either break or bend around the bars sufficiently for their purpose.

Having selected the window which seemed the most favorable, they considered the matter as settled, and then addressed themselves to the study of the prison surroundings, the manner in which it was guarded and other things which they thought it would be useful to know. They desired especially to know something of the topography of the city and they spent much of the day in taking observations from the windows.

Once in the open country, the loyal sun by day and the stars by night would direct their course; for the lights of heaven do not look with favor upon secession, which is something unknown to the celestial sphere.

During the evening and all night long, the two prisoners, in the silence and darkness of their room, watched and listened, taking note of everything that occurred without the walls. They observed when the sound of passing feet and wheels ceased in the street; when the lamps were lighted; when the city seemed generally to have sunk to repose; when the lamps were extinguished, and at what time in the morning the hurrying stream of life began to flow again. They noticed also the sentinel's beat, and calculated that, if they did not attract his attention by any noise made in their descent, they would have ample time to reach the ground and steal away from the immediate vicinity of the prison before he could pass twice over the space he was required to traverse.

At an early hour in the morning, they retired to rest, but not with any intention of dreaming, and slept soundly till breakfast time.

During the forenoon, they discussed together the route it would be advisable for them to take. They could either go down the peninsula and attempt to reach Fortress Monroe, or they could move almost directly northward toward Aquia Creek. There was but little difference in distance; the only question was, which is the safer route. They knew our troops had abandoned the peninsula and supposed the ground to be occupied by the rebels.

"If it is," said Staples, "we shall stand a right smart chance of being taken and returned to this hotel."

On the other hand if, as they suspected, a large part of the rebel army had gone north, it seemed probable that it had gone northward toward Aquia Creek, to which place from Richmond, there was an almost straight line of railroad. To take this route seemed, at first glance, to be running after the enemy with a certainty of being captured;

but further consideration convinced them that the Confederate troops would be moved by rail and that if they bore to the right and kept off from the line of railroad, they would have little to fear, except from occasional cavalry parties and the inhabitants of the country through which they would have to pass. These they thought they could avoid by keeping to the fields and woods instead of the highways, and traveling mostly by night.

They finally determined to make their march to freedom by this route. Staples proposed to start that night. Lyon was no less eager to be gone, but he did not like to depart until he had once more seen Heloise and taken some sort of farewell.

That afternoon the lady came again, accompanied as usual by her faithful Cæsar, and while Staples extracted from the latter all the information of which he was possessed in regard to the topography of the city and the disposition of rebel troops, Captain Lyon engaged the mistress in conversation.

"But for your visits, Heloise, this life would be unendurable."

"Scarcely endurable, as it is, I fear," returned she.

"While you are present it is easily endurable, but I confess to you that I loathe this inactivity."

"You may be exchanged soon."

"And when I am gone, will you be able to remember me till the war closes?"

"Perhaps, if it closes soon; but if it should prove a thirty years war, who can vouch for memory then?"

"This war cannot last like that; it is on too large a scale to be protracted many years. It must end soon."

"Then I will try to remember you," said she smiling: "but I warn you not to grow gray in service and yet expect to live young and fresh in my memory."

"But give me my liberty, and then if hard fighting on

my part can bring peace and Heloise, you may count on a speedy end of the war."

"I see you are determined to throw your life away at the first chance. But we will keep you prisoner here where you are safe, my brave Captain. You are not gone yet."

"And yet I may be, within a week.

"What? why do you speak so?" said she gazing inquiringly upon his animated features.

"As you just said, I may be exchanged."

"True; but I hope not; at least I fear—I dread the danger you will go to."

"Fear not but hope and pray for me, and tell me now, that when I am struggling in my country's service I may count upon your constancy."

"You may," responded she with trembling voice.

Filled with undefined alarms, her cheeks flushed and her eyes grew misty. She could not tell the cause of such sudden, vague fears, but when they came to part and their hands met as good-bye was said, she felt as though she should not look upon him again. He knew that he was gazing upon her face for the last time for months—perhaps for years—if ever he should see her again.

CHAPTER VIII.

DIGGING OUT—EXIT FROM LIBBY—UNEXPECTED ENCOUNTER AND REINFORCEMENT—THE MARCH TO FREEDOM BEGUN—THE DESERTED CABIN—A CALL FROM CONFEDERATE TROOPERS—THE RETREAT RESUMED ON HORSEBACK—DANGER AHEAD—A HORSE TRADE—CÆSAR APPOINTED COMMISSARY—CONFISCATION OF REBEL PROPERTY AND A NARROW ESCAPE.

THAT evening after tea the prisoners sat down by the window and proceeded noiselessly to pick away with their knives the masonry, which secured the bars in place. It was very slow work, but they kept steadily at it, except when they heard steps beneath their window. As the night wore on, and there was less danger of their operations being heard and discovered, they worked more energetically, and had the satisfaction of seeing that they were making some progress, although their knives gave evidence that they were not designed to cut anything quite so hard as the walls of Libby prison.

By midnight each had succeeded in loosening the end of a bar, and applying their united strength they bent them around. From their bed-blankets they constructed a rope which was long enough to reach within easy dropping distance of the ground. Next they removed the lower part of the window, and the way was open. Then they waited until they saw the sentinel pass under their window and turn the corner of the building all unsuspicious of the fast beating hearts above him and the plot which was about to be put in execution against the peace and dignity of the Confederacy.

"Now is our time; not a moment is to be lost," whispered Lyon excitedly. "Go first if you choose."

Staples grasped the cord, one end of which had been secured, and crawling through the opening, slid swiftly down and dropped lightly to the ground.

One moment Lyon waited to see if any alarm was raised, and then he rapidly followed his friend and soon stood by his side.

As silently as possible they fled down the street in the opposite direction from that which the sentinel had taken. They had passed over not more than half a block when a dark figure sprang from the shadow of a building on to the sidewalk directly in front of them.

Lyon drew back his arm to level this obstacle to his progress, when the unknown, seeing his peril, spoke in a loud whisper—

"Don't strike, Massa Lyon; it's Cæsar—I'se been watchin' for you. Miss Heloise tole me. Come wid me; carriage 'round de corner."

While giving utterance to these ejaculations, Cæsar was rapidly leading the way to the carriage he had spoken of, which stood but a few rods distant in charge of a fellow servant.

The faithful black quickly opened the door and beckoning them to enter whispered as they obeyed him—

"Dere's oder close in dare, wid pistols, knives and eberyting yer want."

They jumped in: the door was shut and Cæsar mounted the box. As the carriage rolled along at a gentle trot, its occupants found each a suit of plain clothes lying on the forward seat, for which they exchanged their own as soon as they could. In the breast pocket of each coat were found a small pair of revolvers and a sheath knife, together with a box of ball cartridges.

"My dream is coming true I think," said Staples as they were making these discoveries, and effecting an exchange of garments.

"It is indeed. Miss Wolfe must have suspected our design, though I did not intend to give her cause."

"Women are quicker-witted than men. She interpreted correctly your lugubrious expression at parting, and sent Cæsar, as he informed us, with the carriage to wait for our exit from Libby."

They were soon off the pavement and then the horses were put to a smarter gait. After about an hour's ride they stopped. Cæsar opened the door and the two fugitives stepping out found themselves on a country road and a few miles distant southward from Richmond.

Cæsar explained that he had driven them there to avoid the rebel troops, which were most to the north of the city, and then addressing himself to Lyon he said:

"Massa Lyon, Miss Heloise say I can go wid you if yer chooses. I knows all de country, and de niggers on de way won't be afraid of me, ef we want to get sumting for de inner man, as massa Will say. 'Sides, ef we hab to help ourselbes, I don't show so well in de dark as a white man. When I comes under de hen-roost, golly! de chickens on'y tinks it's gettin a little more cloudy and dey put deyr heads under toder wing and goes right to sleep agin."

"You would, no doubt, be a great help to us Cæsar, but I don't like to expose you to the danger of capture."

"Miss Heloise tinks I had better go," returned Cæsar, who evidently knew his mistress' mind and seemed anxious to gratify her wishes at whatever cost to himself.

"Your mistress is an angel!" exclaimed Staples enthusiastically.

"Sartin sure; massa Staples right dis time ebery bit!" said Cæsar, exhibiting such specimens of nature's dentistry as would have excited wild envy in the breast of the king of beasts.

"I move that we take Cæsar along," said Staples; "Miss Wolfe has planned well for us thus far."

"It seems to be her wish and shall be heeded; but we must protect him, her faithful servant, with our lives if necessary. Cæsar, you may go with us," said Lyon.

"Tank, you, massa Captain," returned the slave, grinning with delight, not at the prospect of freedom, of which he thought little, but at the dignity of his new position, and the knowledge that his young mistress would be pleased with the faithful service which he meant to perform.

"Hopes we won't meet massa Will dough," he muttered to himself.

The cast-off uniforms were taken out of the carriage and concealed. Cæsar took from under the driver's seat a small valise well filled with provisions, and from his pocket a roll of confederate bills, which latter he handed to Lyon, whom he seemed to regard as his master. The carriage was then sent back in charge of the other servant, with a verbal message to his mistress, and the two young officers under the guidance of Cæsar set out to find the army of the Potomac.

They made a wide detour around Richmond, moving first in a northwesterly direction and avoiding the travelled roads as much as possible. They crossed the James in a row-boat, which Cæsar knew exactly where to look for, and then bearing to the right they approached the railroad. They did this with some trepidation, but trusting to the friendly darkness and celerity of movement, they went forward. There were no habitations in their neighborhood, but as they neared the track they heard a whistle and the thunder of an approaching train. Looking north they saw the head-light of an engine, like a ball of fire in the distance, and throwing themselves flat upon the ground they waited for it.

"Hope they won't stop for passengers at this station," said Staples.

The train came up and passed by. The cars were filled with soldiers, and by the light within, some bandaged heads were visible.

"There has been a battle." said Lyon, "and they are taking to Richmond the wounded that are able to be moved."

"Yes; and perhaps a few prisoners also," said Staples. "Well, we have made a little room for them by evacuating our quarters."

As the train disappeared, the three men rose to their feet, and dashing across the track they turned their faces to the northeast and walked rapidly along, feeling that every step took them farther from the dangerous vicinity of the railroad, farther from Richmond, and nearer to freedom.

They travelled on till daylight appeared, and then finding themselves in a cultivated country where they were likely to meet with people, if they continued their journey by day, they looked about them for some place of concealment.

Remote from any house they found a deserted cabin, the garden about it grown up to weeds, showing that it had not recently been occupied.

They entered it and, securing the door, sat down to rest themselves, and partake of a breakfast from the valise, which Cæsar had carried suspended from a stick over his shoulder.

"Staples, do you and Cæsar lie down and sleep; I will keep watch till you have had your nap. It isn't best for us all to be caught napping together."

"Massa Lyon, you sleep first. I will look sharp, said Cæsar.

"No," replied Lyon, who, knowing the propensity of the negro to sleep, did not dare to trust him to keep the first watch. "Go to sleep, Cæsar, as quickly as you can; you will need all you can get."

Without further remonstrance, the negro and Staples stretched themselves on the floor and were soon fast asleep.

Lyon kept a lookout over the surrounding country, while his mind was busy with grateful and tender thoughts of Heloise, and with speculations regarding the success likely to attend his present endeavor. He saw people at a distance, mostly blacks, attending to their usual avocations, but no one approached the hiding-place of himself and companions.

About eleven o'clock, he touched Staples lightly: The "Darty" opened his eyes, and taking in the situation rose to his feet. Cæsar still slept the sleep of innocence, though making a fiendish noise in so doing.

"Better let him sleep," whispered Lyon, "He can't endure the fatigue that we can, and I don't like to trust my safety to the watchfulness of a sleepy nigger."

Staples nodded and took up his position at the little window, while Lyon took possession of his vacant couch and was soon sleeping as soundly as Cæsar himself.

During the remainder of the long day, Staples remained on guard. Impatiently he watched the slow motion of the sun as it rolled down the western slope of the sky. It seemed to him to move more slowly down its inclined plane than he had ever seen it before, as though the amount of friction it had to overcome was almost insuperable. His eagerness for the shades of night grew feverish as the afternoon wore on so lingeringly.

At last, just before sunset, he observed a party of four cavalrymen ride up to the nearest mansion, less than half a mile distant. They remained sometime, apparently in conversation with the planter, and then Staples saw them turn and ride away. He watched them intently, and soon, to his dismay, saw them halt and, after a short parley, turn their horses' heads in the direction of the cabin.

On they came directly towards him, though not with any haste or apparent motive, and he trusted that they would pass by. But no—they rode up within a few rods of the door, and noticing the fresh footsteps around it, they halted.

The noise awoke Lyon. He sprang up, and one glance showed him the state of affairs. Immediately he woke Cæsar, bidding him in a whisper to be silent. When that individual comprehended their condition, a gray pallor diffused itself over his countenance, giving him an unearthly appearance.

A shout was heard from those without, designed to attract the attention of the inmates.

No answer was returned, as the occupants of the cabin could not at once decide what course it was best to pursue.

But when two of the troopers dismounted, as though to enter, Lyon saw there was no more time for hesitation.

"Throw off your coat, leave your cap and go out as though you lived here," he said to Cæsar, "and get them away if possible."

The faithful fellow immediately obeyed and ran out of the door in seeming haste to answer the summons.

"There you are, eh? just woke up have you? Who lives here?"

"I does, sah." replied Cæsar.

"All alone?"

"No sah: my ole mamma."

"Now nigger look a here: have you seen a couple of white men—strangers—around here to day."

"No, massa."

"If I catch you lying. I'll skin you."

"Lets go in and look," said another. "It don't appear as if anybody had lived here before to-day."

"De ole woman berry sick," said Cæsar, trembling with apprehension.

"Hold the horses, you black rascal, never mind the old woman."

Cæsar took the horses and the two men rudely pushed open the door and swaggered into the cabin. Lyon and Staples stood behind the door as it swung in, and as their unwelcome visitors entered the dimly lighted apartment, they quickly closed it again and each springing at one of the astonished rebels, they dealt such tremendous blows that both intruders were brought senseless to the floor.

The noise was heard outside.

"It's de dog I'se afeard," cried Cæsar; "he neber barks."

The other two men sprang from their horses, which Cæsar also grasped, and breathing curses upon him and his dog, they rushed with drawn swords to the door. The first to cross the threshold received a blow from Staples' dagger which made him fall backward out of the doorway, and Lyon leaping over his body seized the fourth paralyzed trooper with a vice-like grip by the throat and hurled him like a log, stunned and bleeding, to the earth.

It was growing dusky and this struggle had been so brief and silent that no attention had been attracted to it.

"To horse!" said Lyon mounting one and taking a second by the bridle. Staples and Cæsar followed his example and in less than a minute the three were riding rapidly away with the four horses, their heads turned due north.

There was no pursuit, but they rode as though Stuart's entire cavalry force was close in their rear. The roads were good and by midnight they had left the scene of their last adventure far behind them.

Staples' horse beginning to show signs of exhaustion and a disinclination to keep up with the rest, the Captain removed his bridle and other trappings and turned him adrift. Then mounting the led horse the party pushed on again, though at a somewhat slower rate, owing to the fatigue of the horses, the increasing darkness, and the unevenness of the country.

After another hour's ride, as they reached the top of a slight acclivity and looked before them, they saw at half a mile's distance what seemed to be the light of a camp fire.

"Are we trapped again?" inquired Staples as they halted.

"There seems to be a trap there, but we need not step into it unless we choose," replied Lyon.

"Golly! dis nigger will be killed shuah," soliloquized Cæsar.

"It is probably a small foraging party," continued Lyon. "Shall we go nearer and satisfy our curiosity?"

"I don't see the necessity of it," returned his companion. "Never throw stones at a hornet's nest. Let us move quietly around them at a safe distance."

In accordance with this prudent counsel they bore to the right, describing a semi-circle to avoid the rebel encampment. As they came opposite it, the necessities of the ground forced them to approach nearer than they liked, but they were rewarded for the extra danger by coming upon a place where half a dozen horses were tethered. Silently dismounting and finding that the animals were much better and fresher than their own, they selected three of the best, bridled and mounted them and turning the others loose, together with their own jaded beasts, they rode on again at a walk till they were at a safer distance, and then once more galloped along, highly pleased with their horse trade, which was about as honest a transaction of its sort as is often seen.

Cæsar was so shaken with suppressed mirth that he could hardly keep his seat.

"Hie! yah! yah!" he ejaculated in a gurgling voice, "ef dis a'n't de neatest trick!—Beats eberyting—'spect its legle dough."

On they went at a good rate of speed, directing their course by the stars, and when morning dawned they found themselves in a wooded and rough country, and with their horses pretty nearly used up.

They turned from the road they had been following and rode slowly, as they were obliged to, into a dense forest. Here, after removing the bridles, which they thought best to retain, they abandaned their horses and then climbed on foot up the steep of a mountain, till they had gained a situation where they thought they were not likely to be discovered.

Crawling under the branches of some low trees, which grew at the base of a large rock where they found a spring of water, they threw their tired bodies on the ground. Having satisfied their thirst and devoured the remainder of Cæsar's store of provisions, they all lay down to sleep, not thinking it necessary for either to remain on guard.

Weary, as they were, they slept soundly till past noon. Waking at last, they refreshed themselves again at the spring, washing their hands and faces in the clear, cool water. then crawling out of their lair, they set out on foot through the woods and travelled as fast as the obstructions they met with would permit.

All the afternoon they kept in the shelter of the woods, but as the sun sank out of sight they emerged therefrom and found themselves in the neighborhood of a large plantation, whose extensive negro quarters evinced the wealth and importance of the proprietor, and afforded a visible cause of the rebellion.

They were hungry and they constituted themselves a committee of ways and means.

It was now Cæsar's opportunity to make himself eminently useful to his beloved mistress's friend, and he exhibited his readiness to improve it.

"I knows jes' whar de chickens roost in such a place as dat, and I tink ef I goes to de quarters de colored folks will gib me what I wants ef I tell dem I'se runnin away to de norf."

"I think you can help us now Cæsar, said Lyon; "we must let you try at all events."

They waited till the lights were all extinguished in the "great house," and then all three proceeded cautiously to within a short distance of the negro quarters, where Lyon gave Cæsar his final instructions.

"You know your people best, and you may either throw yourself on their generosity or help yourself as you see fit. We will wait for you here. If you are molested, use your pistols if necessary and fight your way back to us through everything. We will come to your aid if you need it. Be careful and be quick, and say nothing about us. Let them think you are alone."

Thus charged, Cæsar set off, while Lyon and Staples sat down to wait for him; though not without considerable anxiety.

"I feel like a rat fooling around a trap after a bit of cheese," remarked Staples.

"We run a risk, I know," returned his companion, "but we must have something to eat."

In about half an hour Cæsar returned with a well filled sack over his shoulder.

"I've got it," he said gleefully, "and dere's hosses in de stable."

"Fortune seems to favor us," said Staples eagerly; "I move we take them."

"Agreed," said Lyon, and they proceeded, led by Cæsar, to the stables.

Each selected a horse out of a well filled stable and led him out. They were spirited animals and made so much disturbance, plunging and snorting, while they were being got in readiness, that the family was aroused. Lights began to move in the house; the negroes to flock out, and two white men soon appeared upon the scene, without coats or hats, one of them carrying a gun and the other a lantern.

"What's the matter here?" cried the older, hurrying into the midst of the excitement.

There was a confused murmur of negro voices but no intelligible answer.

As the lantern flashed upon our hero and his companions, who were mounting the horses, the planter seemed to understand the matter.

"A robbery! and my best horses, too! Get down you villains, or I'll blow you to pieces. Off! I say."

He drew up his gun.

"Off, it is—we're going sir," cried Lyon, upon whom the weapon was now brought to bear.

Striking the fiery steed with his boots, he plunged him against the enraged planter, bearing him to the ground before he could fire, and sending a bullet from his pistol through the lantern held by the other man, he fled like the wind through the yielding and helpless crowd of negroes, with Staples and Cæsar following close behind him at the same furious speed.

They were not to get away without a parting volley, however.

The man who had borne the lantern seized the musket as it fell from the hand of the overthrown planter and fired at random after the fugitives.

There was a rattle of glass in the sack which Cæsar carried and a yell of dismay from the sable trooper.

"Are you hurt?" cried Lyon, checking his horse.

"No massa," he answered as he darted past the captain, like a thunder cloud on horse back, " but de bottle am broke, I reckon."

"Forward! then" shouted Staples, "and hang on to that bag."

Forward they sped, while excited orders to mount and pursue them were heard in their rear.

They felt satisfied that the best horses on the plantation were under them, and they laughed at pursuit as they dashed ahead.

CHAPTER IX.

COL. WOLFE AT HOME—HIS DISCOVERY—PRIVATE WAIT ON GUARD—AN ALARM AND UNEXPECTED ARRIVAL FROM RICHMOND—CAPT. LYON JOINS HIS REGIMENT—THE ARMY MOVES DOWN THE RAPPAHANNOCK—THE BATTLE OF FREDERICKSBURG.

HEN Col. Wolfe had bidden farewell to his friend Lyon in Libby Prison, he immediately joined his regiment and set out for the north with the main body of the rebel army. The intention was to crush Pope, who had been given the command of what was called the Army of Virginia out of courtesy to Gen. McClellan, who was supposed to be in command of the Army of the Potomac. But Gen. Pope's advancement was virtually a superseding of Gen. McClellan, who had lost the confidence of the administration by his disastrous Peninsular Campaign; for Halleck was appointed General-in Chief, and as such ordered McClellan to support Pope, who had been assigned the duty of covering Washington and protecting Maryland with its great railroad, while threatening Richmond from the north.

In the latter days of August, 1862, was fought the second battle on the fated field of Bull Run, while Lyon was a prisoner in Richmond. In the prescience of God it was, like the first battle, recognized as a defeat to the Union arms, and defeat it became. Whether it was made such by unworthy instruments is a question for historians, rather than romance writers, to discuss.

In the battle, young Wolfe distinguished himself by his bravery and did his full share of service in obscuring the glory of Gen. Pope.

Pope's army was almost entirely demolished, and now in obedience to the demand of a large majority of the officers and soldiers of the army of the Potomac, whose confidence in their former leader was still unshaken, Gen. McClellan was re-invested with the chief command.

After several minor conflicts, the battle of Antietam was fought on Sept. 17,—" the bloodiest day that America ever saw." The battle was a victory to the North, but dearly purchased and not at all decisive. We held the ground, but Lee retired strong enough to fight some other day.

In this battle, the reckless Wolfe was severely wounded, and sent back to Richmond to recover. He was on board the very train which had passed the three fugitives on the night of their escape from Richmond.

When the Colonel learned from his sister of the escape of his friend from prison, he was much surprised, but he could not help showing a certain satisfaction at hearing of his old chum's daring exploit. Heloise did not think him very sorry that Lyon had not been re-captured. When he afterward found out that Cæsar had mysteriously disappeared about the same time, a light seemed to break in upon him, and further conversation with his sister made the matter clearer to him. He did not, however, attempt to win her confidence or force her to confession, and at heart he was pleased that his sister had chosen Tom Lyon as the object of her love.

Let us now return with the speed of thought to the North, while our three fugitives are making their way thither on the confiscated horses of the Virginia planter. After the battle of Antietam there was little fighting for a couple of months, for the same number of reasons: Lee was not anxious for a fight and McClellan was too cautious to take any chances. There was a southward movement of the two opposing armies from the bloody soil of Maryland, made in parallel lines and on opposite sides of the Blue Ridge. The latter part of October McClellan occupied Snicker's Gap and Manassas and had advanced as far as Warrenton before his active participation in the war was brought to a close.

The Vermont Brigade showed by its wasted numbers the hard and dangerous service it had seen, and the gallant manner in which it had discharged its duties. Captain Nason had been sent home so severely wounded that he could never draw his sword again. All the others of our old friends had not only survived their perils but had escaped unhurt, but their bronzed faces and the diminished form of private Hank Wait, who had left sixty pounds of his flesh upon the Peninsula, bore witness to the fact that they had not escaped their full share of hardship.

One night, before the southward movement of the army had begun and while it was waiting for the rebel Jeb. Stuart to ride around it, as he had done once before, private Wait was stationed on picket.

"On your care," said Lieut. Joe Safford, addressing Hank, "depends perhaps the safety of the army and the fate of the country. I therefore caution you not to snore as loudly as usual, else you will be likely to attract the attention of the enemy and furnish them a sure guide to our position."

Picket duty is not the most pleasant experience of a soldier's life, and as the hours lagged, as though loth to depart, while nothing occurred to disturb the silence and darkness of the night, Hank's thoughts became anything but cheerful companions, and he began to wish that something would happen to relieve the monotony and prove his vigilance.

The wish was scarcely formed, and not fully endorsed by his better judgment, when he heard footsteps approaching and the sound of voices. As the disturbers of his quiet came nearer and got within what he considered a proper distance, or an improper nearness, he hailed them:

"Who goes there?"

"Friends."

"Halt, friends; let one advance and give the countersign."

There was a halt and when one came forward, speaking as he came—

"We have not the countersign; we are prisoners escaped from the enemy, and wish to be taken into the Union camp."

"Halt! or I fire!" cried Hank, fearing treachery, and bringing his piece to his shoulder.

"If you are not Hank Wait, then I'm a rebel, so ground that musket," returned the threatened stranger, walking rapidly forward instead of obeying the order to halt.

Hank's fears were somewhat relieved by this familiar address, and he permitted the unknown to approach him. When he recognized the voice and form of Capt. Lyon, he dropped his gun and seized his friend with both hands.

"Why, Tom, where did you rain from?"

"From Richmond, and I brought a piece of the cloud along with me. Staples and Cæsar, come," he called to his companions, and they soon appeared.

"This is the cloud, I suppose," said Hank, looking at Cæsar.

In a short time the three fugitives from Rebeldom were among their friends in camp, where they were warmly welcomed. They had to narrate their adventures and were listened to with interest. From their tale it appeared that they reached Aquia Creek a few days after we left them dashing away on the planter's horses, and without any incident worthy of mention. There their dangers ended. Learning the location of their regiments, they resolved to report themselves in camp without delay, and getting transportation up the Potomac they rejoined the army as we have seen.

Soon after this, as we have said, the army began its southward movement, but the advance had got no further than Warrenton, when Gen. McClellan was relieved of the command and ordered home to Trenton, N. J.

Gen. Burnside now succeeded to the command of the army. of the Potomac, Nov. 8, 1862, and immediately commenced to move his forces down the Rappahannock to Fredericksburg. Lee moved his army in a parallel line down the south bank of the river, ready to resist the crossing of the Union troops wherever they should attempt it.

Burnside laid a pontoon across the river to Fredericksburgh and another about two miles below, much of the work being done under the fire of the enemy and at a loss of three hundred men. The city was then cleared of the enemy and a few prisoners taken, and our army, 100,000 strong, had possession of both banks of the river. Lee's army of 80,000 men was posted along the bluffs for a distance of five or six miles, a very advantageous position. Three hundred rebel guns were stationed on the eminences, in a position to rake every part of the ground by which they could be approached. Immediately in the rear of Fredericksburg stood Marye's Hill, which the rebels held and which they had fortified from its base to its summit. At the base was a stone wall behind which was stationed a brigade of infantry, and above this battery rose above battery to the frowning summit, ready to pour down a deadly storm of shot upon our advancing columns.

Burnside certainly showed himself unfit for command when he ordered his brave men to certain death that there awaited them; but he gave the command and on the 13th day of December the attack began. The brave Irish Brigade under Gen. Meagher dashed itself six times against that fiery hill, and of the 1200 men led into action but 280 appeared on parade next morning. But the slaughter of the gallant Irishmen was useless, for the position could not be carried.

The fighting was not all at this point, however. Reynolds and Meade engaged the enemy on the left, farther down the river, and the Vermont Brigade crossed the lower pontoon to take part in the conflict which raged in the neighborhood of Lee's headquarters.

The rebel cavalry came into action here, and the famous Black Horse Cavalry, which made itself a name at the first battle of Bull Run, hurled itself against the steady front of the Green Mountain Boys. Men and horses were mingled in wild confusion; swords and bayonets dripping with blood flashed in the sunlight; shouts and groans and the reports of muskets and pistols filled the air.

"Make infantry of them," cried private Wait as he bayoneted a horse and proceeded to knock its rider on the head.

His advice and example being followed, there were more horseless riders than riderless horses that escaped from the field. Most of the shots fired were aimed at the horses, and when, after a desperate but unsuccessful attempt to throw the Old Brigade into confusion, the enemy withdrew. There were scores of horses left behind never to be ridden into battle again.

"I'm afraid black horses will get scarce in Virginia if they ain't more careful of them," said Hank, as his company re-formed its rather uneven line, and in obedience to command turned to meet and overcome new dangers.

Thus all day long the battle raged in different parts of the extensive field. Sometimes success at particular points waited on our arms, but the result of the entire conflict was greatly against us. It was a defeat to the Union army, and when night closed the slaughter, we had lost 15,000 men and gained not one inch of ground, or any material advantage.

Burnside's attempt had proved a bloody and costly failure. For the next two days the two hostile armies stood facing each other, neither daring to attack, and then our army was withdrawn to the north bank of the river, and Fredericksburg abandoned.

On the return of the troops, Cæsar, who had prudently refrained from crossing the river, made his appearance among his friends and seemed pleased to find them unharmed.

"Ain't you sorry you didn't go over, Cæsar?" inquired Hank.

"Not berry, sah; de air am more salubricarious on dis side."

"But there was a chance to win glory," persisted Hank.

"Neber cared for sich tings," replied Cæsar, loftily.

"Weren't you just a little afraid of being shot?"

"No, sah; not 'fraid; but Ise wuf money, an' my missis tole me to be careful ob myself. White men don't cos' nuffin, and won't sell for nuffin, but when you shoot me, dere's a tousan' dollars frowed away."

"It's just as well, my colored friend, that you didn't risk your precious form," said Dr. Safford, who happened to be passing by; "for there wasn't glory enough to go around among the white men. Our captain, your master, took the lion's share, which was quite natural and proper for a Lyon to do."

L

The pontoons were taken up—the enemy re occupied Fredericksburg, and hostilities were reduced to picket-firing across the river.

Capt. Lyon had distinguished himself by his coolness and bravery and was soon after promoted to major.

Burnside's usefulness as commander of the army of the Potomac was at an end, and he was soon after released from the command, though he was on the eve of putting in execution a new plan for the capture of Richmond.

Nearly all our commanders seemed to labor under and to be governed by the impression that the taking of Richmond would prove the end of the rebellion, while to a non-military mind it appears that the mere capture of that city would have resulted in nothing more serious to the rebel cause than the necessity of removing the rebel government to some other locality. Time proved that the only practical method of conquering the Confederacy was to wear it out— to kill, wound and take prisoners its fighting men, to deplete its treasury and ruin its credit—to cripple all its resources so that it could no longer keep an effective army in the field. Every rebel soldier disabled for service, every thousand dollars spent in equipping an army for the field, every week of time during which they were obliged to maintain their cause at great expense, helped on the final consummation. When men and money and needful supplies began to grow scarce, the rebellion, which had been a mere shell for some time, suddenly collapsed. So long as an effective blockade was kept up, it didn't matter much where the fighting was done, if only it was done.

CHAPTER X.

CHANCELLORSVILLE AND GETTYSBURG—STANNARD'S BRIGADE—OUR HEROES MEET AGAIN IN BATTLE—STAPLES TURNS THE TIDE—CÆSAR SEEKS HIS WOUNDED MASTER ON THE FIELD—THE SLAVE'S AFFECTION FOR HIS MASTER—A MYSTERY TO PRIVATE WAIT IN HOSPITAL—CONVALESCENT—A SURPRISE.

GEN. Hooker assumed command of the army of the Potomac, Jan. 26th, 1863. The army was in a bad condition. The men were disheartened by the disasters they had suffered and desertions were frequent. General Hooker wisely spent two months in disciplining and inspiriting his troops and with such success that at the end of that time he had an army of 123,000 men, who had confidence in their general and were ready once more to meet the foe. The battle of Chancellorsville, which was to try their courage, was fought on nearly the same field as that of Fredericksburg, the scene of their late defeat.

Gen. Hooker mapped his intended movement so well that he succeeded in crossing the Rappahannock without any loss or opposition whatever. He was confident of victory, and declared that he held Lee's army in one hand and Richmond in the other. Seven days elapsed from the crossing to the re-crossing of the river—days filled up with important movements and heavy fighting. The first collision was rather to the advantage of the rebels. The next day Stonewall Jackson with 25,000 men, having greatly changed his position by marching all day and concealing his movements from observation, appeared in a part of the field where he was not expected, and suddenly emerging from the woods he burst upon the 11th corps near nightfall, routing it and scattering the panic stricken fugitives, who carried dismay wherever they fled with their tidings of disaster. Pouring down the Chancellorsville road they threatened to infect the whole army with the fright which possessed them.

Pleasanton, with his artillery, arrested the tide of disaster which threatened to engulf all. Ordering Major Keenan with 500 men to charge the rebel 25,000, which he did at the cost of his life ten minutes after, Pleasanton had time to get his guns in position and double-shotted. Three times the rebels charged upon him—once to within fifty yards of his guns—but each time they were repulsed with tremendous slaughter.

In this engagement Stonewall Jackson fell mortally wounded, between nine and ten o'clock at night, and Pleasanton, supported by Sickles' infantry, was left master of the position.

All night operations continued. At midnight Gen. Sickles advanced a division and ordered a charge down the plank road, which drove back the rebels and recovered a part of the ground lost by rout of the 11th corps. At daylight, however, he was ordered by Hooker to fall back on Chancellorsville, which he did slowly and without loss, although closely followed by the enemy.

It was Sunday, May 3d, and the rebels, led by J. E. B. Stuart, dashed themselves upon Sickles' corps with such gallantry and utter recklessness of life that they deserved success, if gallantry alone can ever deserve it. Up to the very mouths of our cannon they charged, but the discharge from forty guns, ably handled, cut frightful swaths through their close ranks. The Union troops fought them until their ammunition was exhausted, and then repelled five fierce charges with their bayonets. A message was then sent to headquarters for relief, but in vain, as Hooker had been rendered insensible by a cannon ball, which struck a pillar of the Chancellorsville house, against which he was leaning. The hard pressed corps was forced to fall back and soon the whole army was withdrawn a mile northward, leaving Chancellorsville to the enemy.

The fight was nearly all over in this part, but Sedgwick, who had crossed the river two or three miles below Fredericksburg, with the intention of falling on Lee's rear and crushing the rebel army between himself and Hooker, now renewed the contest, which raged as fiercely as before.

The Vermont Brigade, belonging to the 6th corps, was with Sedgwick. Maj. Lyon was in command of his regiment, in the absence of any superior officer. The troops began their march from the pontoons at night, and fighting every inch of the way, entered Fredericksburg at daylight Monday morning.

The rebel troops were concentrated on Marye's hill, which Burnside had vainly attempted to carry in the former battle, and where the Irish Brigade had been sacrificed.

The first attempt to clear the rifle-pits at the foot of the hill was repulsed, and another plan was resolved upon. Just before noon three storming columns, one of them led by Maj. Lyon and composed entirely of Green Mountain Boys, advanced with resolute step against Cemetery hill, which it was thought best to attack first.

Under a heavy fire of artillery they charged up the hill without halting or wavering. Closing up their ranks as often as they were broken by the fire they sustained, they pushed on with determined faces, and eyes fixed on the summit of that hill as the goal they must reach.

"Steady, boys! forward!" cried Lyon at every discharge of lead which rained upon them.

The very tone of his voice gave assurance that the order would be obeyed. Up the height they rushed, our hero at their head, while the tall form of Lieut. Joe Safford kept close in his rear like an elongation of his shadow.

"This is worse than climbing Atherton's hill, after the cows," cooly remarked Joe, referring to the home cow-pasture.

"I wish I was there, though," said Hank, who was in the front rank and heard the remark. "I'd rather swallow raspberries, with the worms on, than these cannon balls."

Still upward they pressed with unabated courage till only a few yards separated them from the enemy.

"Upon them, boys!" shouted Lyon, waving his sword and dashing upon the rebel gunners as though he had been shot from a mortar.

His sword flashed and writhed like a fiery serpent and death followed its every stroke. His men swarmed after him over the crest of the hill and a few seconds decided the question of mastery. The fight was won, and 200 prisoners with guns and camp equipage fell into the hands of the victors. A rousing cheer announced the fact to all concerned.

But the victory was not gained without cost. That bloody slope—fitly named cemetery hill—was scattered over with the dead bodies of brave men, and in the very moment of triumph the gallant Safford sank down on the height, severely wounded.

But there was no time to mourn for the dead, and scarce any to care for the wounded. Hank was permitted to remain behind to care for his old school-mate and boyhood's friend, Lieut. Joe, and the storming column rushed on against Marye's hill like a resistless wave at floodtide, bearing all before it.

The second height was taken like the first, and glory rested on the banners of the Old Brigade.

Still onward rushed Sedgwick's victorious corps on the track of the retiring rebels for three or four miles, when the latter halted and gave battle. Their position proved too strong to be carried, and when Lee, having compelled Hooker to retire from his front, turned the bulk of his army upon Sedgwick, our troops were forced back before the superior force brought against them, and finally during the night Sedgwick was obliged to retreat across the river with heavy loss.

The next night Hooker himself crossed to the north side of the river with the balance of our army and the battle of Chancellorsville was ended. The losses of the enemy were doubtless as great as our own, but for the second time they had driven us across the Rhappahannock, and with some show of reason they claimed the victory.

Our hero, for gallant conduct, was promoted to the rank of colonel, and Hank would have been ennobled by being raised to the rank of corporal, but he distinctly declined the honor.

"I ain't ambitious," said he; "I don't hanker after office. In my humble sphere I am content to remain and do my duty to my country; but who knows what might happen if I should accept promotion? I might not be satisfied till I had got to be general-in-chief, and had ruined my country by proving the destroyer of its liberty. Napoleon was spoiled by being a corporal. If he hadn't been corporal, he never would have been general or emperor, and the population of the earth would have been considerably greater than it is now. If he had always been a private soldier, the blood spilled to gratify his ambition would have been happily saved to the world and permitted to flow in peaceful streams through the veins of quiet citizens. I don't want to be a second Napoleon, and I won't. Through love of country I turn my back on this temptation. All I ask in return is that hereafter a grateful people shall chisel upon my gravestone—'Hank Wait, private. A patriot rests here.'"

Lieut. Safford's wounds were not mortal, but they were such as to incapacitate him for service, at least for a while. Under the care of his brother, the doctor, he grew strong enough to make the journey to Vermont, and he was sent home to complete his recovery with the hope of a speedy return.

A month of inaction ensued, and then Lee put his army in motion for an invasion of Maryland and Pennsylvania. When it became evident that an important movement was going on, there was considerable skirmishing and some engagements but no great battle.

The rebel army, passing up the south bank of the Rappahannock, crossed the Blue Ridge into the Shenandoah valley and moved northward, taking Winchester in the way, threatening Harper's Ferry and even Washington, before Hooker began to move in force. The rebels had a week the start, and fording the Potomac they struck across Maryland and up as far as Chambersburg, Pa., without meeting any serious opposition.

On the eve of the great battle, Hooker and Halleck disagreed in regard to the propriety of holding Harper's Ferry, and Hooker, at his own request, was relieved of the command, and Gen. Meade was appointed his successor, taking command of the army June 28th, 1863.

Gettysburg, Pa., was a village of 3,000 inhabitants, and there Lee concentrated his army, and there the battle was fought, although Meade had maneuvered at a point some fifteen miles southeast of there.

It is not our purpose to give a detailed account of the battle, which is a matter of history, but to relate those incidents of it in which our characters were concerned.

The part which the troops of Vermont took in this decisive battle reflects credit upon them, and is a matter of just pride to the State which sent them into the field.

The 2d brigade of Vermonters, composed of the 12th, 13th, 14th, 15th and 16th regiments, 9 months men, under Gen. Stannard, performed the most gallant service, and in the opinion of Major Gen. Doubleday the country is mainly indebted to them for the final victory of the third of July.

Two different times charging on the flank of advancing rebel columns, they scooped them *en masse* into our lines, and the 16th regiment, Col. Veazey, in the last charge, captured from the enemy the colors of their regiments. Although it was to most of them their first battle, they fought with the coolness of veterans. Their movements were executed in the open field, under heavy fire and with the promptness and decision of batallion drill. They ended the contest in the center and substantially closed the battle. General Stannard himself was badly wounded, but refused to leave the field until the contest was over.

The Old Brigade, of which Lyon's regiment formed a part, was with the rest of the 6th corps at Manchester, thirty miles away, on July 1st. Receiving orders, they began their march for Gettysburg at 7 p. m. They passed over a rough and hilly country, marching as long as they could see to do so to any advantage, and finally halted on a mountain side to rest and wait for daylight. Their rations were nearly exhausted, but the spirits of the men, inured to hardship, were lively and hopeful.

Officers and men threw themselves down together, wherever they halted, and partook of such refreshments as their haversacks afforded. Col. Lyon, Captain Merritt, and Dr Safford and Hank sat down together.

"Supper is ready, gentlemen." said Hank, producing his last hardtack. "This is the first course, just to give you an appetite for what isn't likely to follow. Have a bite Colonel?"

The Colonel declined, as did his companions, and Hank disposed of the whole first course without any seeming difficulty, but did not seem quite surfeited.

"Doctor," he requested, be so kind as to help me to a portion of that turkey in front of you—the second joint please."

"Pray restrain your voracity, private Wait, returned the doctor. "As your physician, I feel it my duty to warn you against overloading your stomach. Overeating is the curse of the country and is making a nation of dyspeptics. According to such medical authorities as Dr. Dio Starvem, a single hardtack, such as you have just devoured with such improper haste, is quite as much nourishment as any man ought to receive after 12 o'clock noon."

"Thank you doctor; I am very glad I haven't eaten any more, and I hope you will continue to look carefully after my health. I shall write to my mother in regard to your kindness, and I doubt not her anxiety will be much relieved."

"It would, I think, have been much better if you had eaten nothing at all at this hour of the night."

"Give me an emetic, doctor, and I will be more careful after this."

"I hope," said Merritt, "that Dr. Starvem won't be appointed commissary general; but to change the subject from eating, of which there is little to do, to fighting, of which we have always had enough, what do you think, Colonel, is the prospect of our being in season to have a hand in the expected battle?"

"The prospect is dark. I am afraid we shall be late for the main battle, but there will probably be work for us when we get there. I never knew the Old Brigade to fall short of its full share."

"We shall be on the move as soon as it is light enough," said the doctor, "and if you have any respect for my judgment, you will stop talking and stop thinking if possible, and get all the sleep you can."

"Your views in regard to sleep, though not quite so novel to me as those you have expressed in regard to diet, appear to be equally correct, and I shall govern myself accordingly," said Hank, stretching himself on the hillside at an angle of forty-five degrees with the plane of the horizon.

"I advise you," he continued, after some efforts to neutralize the force of gravity which was drawing him down the inclined plane of his earthly couch, "to stick your toes well into the ground if you don't wish to find yourselves at the foot of the hill in the morning."

The tired soldiers were soon asleep, and slept soundly in spite of their uncomfortable lodgings till daylight roused them to resume their march to the field, where the work of death was already going on.

They arrived at Gettysburg, weary enough, in the afternoon of the second day and were soon after thrown into the conflict.

Col. Lyon's regiment was ordered to the front to relieve a regiment which had exhausted its ammunition, and at the same time on the rebel side, Col. Wolfe and his regiment of Georgians was ordered on to the field for a similar reason.

As the opposing troops were but a short distance apart, Wolfe recognized his old friend and held his hat aloft on his sword-point to attract attention. Lyon saw and courteously saluted him, and then these almost brothers began their fight.

It was Georgia against Vermont, and both sides were determined to win. The Norwich Cadets met now for the second time in battle, and neither of them had the slightest idea of yielding to the other.

Volley after volley was exchanged, and men fell on both sides. Lyon received a bullet through his right hand; seizing his sword in his left, he still encouraged his men.

"Charge, Georgians!" cried Wolfe, and at the word his men sprang forward with deafening yells.

The order was plainly heard by the northerners.

"Charge, Vermonters!" cried Lyon, before the former order had fairly died away, and waving his sword he rushed at the head of his ready followers to meet the coming wave. The combatants met with a shock and were mingled in a contest at close quarters.

The two friends avoided each other, but they spared no others.

"Down with them!" exclaimed Lyon, cheering on his men as, bleeding from his wounds, he fought left-handed with deadly effect against all who opposed him.

"Down it is," responded Hank, the unpromoted, as his bayonet transfixed a southern captain, whose uplifted sword in another instant would have cleft the colonel's head.

The Georgians, animated by the example of their commander, fought with reckless fury, and as one of them by a sudden bayonet thrust which Hank (who kept close by the side of his wounded colonel) was not quick enough to prevent, though he took a deadly revenge for it, brought Lyon to the ground, it seemed as though the battle would go in Wolfe's favor. He saw his friend fall and rushed to the spot to save his life if possible.

At that critical juncture a New Hampshire regiment appeared upon the scene and Capt. Staples with his company dashed into the midst of the fight. The Georgians were soon scattered—some being taken prisoners—but their colonel, scorning to flee and fighting to the last, was struck senseless to the ground, without having been recognized by Staples.

It was nearly dark and the fighting was ended for the day. The Vermonters bore away the body of their wounded colonel.

Under the skillful treatment of Dr. Safford, Lyon was restored to consciousness and his wounds properly dressed. As soon as he had collected his thoughts he spoke to Cæsar, who with Hank was watching over him, and told him that his young master William, Col. Wolfe, was probably lying on the field of battle either dead or wounded.

The affectionate negro shed tears at this intelligence.

"Massa Lyon, let me go an' find my young massa."

"Yes; go with him, Hank," said Lyon.

Accordingly Hank and Cæsar set out together for the lately contested field, carrying a stretcher with them, and full canteens of water. The evening was sufficiently light and they found their way to the spot without difficulty. Stepping over the dead, both friend and foe, looking in this and that pale upturned face, or stopping to give a drink to some groaning wounded rebel, they sought for the young colonel.

An exclamation from Cæsar brought Hank to his side. He was bending over the senseless form of his master, one side of whose face was covered with blood which had flowed from a wound in the head.

"Oh! de good Lord spare him! Am he dead, massa Wait?"

Hank examined the young officer and decided that he was not dead. He had received an ugly blow on the head, but no necessarily mortal wound was discovered.

Cæsar seemed much relieved when Hank expressed the opinion that his master would live, but the Vermonter could hardly understand the affection of the slave, for one who claimed the ownership of his body and the right to all the fruits of his labor.

"I feel pretty certain," he remarked to himself, rather more than to Cæsar, "that the only stretcher I should furnish to the man who called himself *my* master, would be in the shape of a hempen cord."

Without further delay they carefully raised the wounded man and placed him on the stretcher, and proceeded to carry him within the Union lines. Arriving there in safety with their burden, they placed Wolfe in the care of the surgeons, who succeeded in restoring him to consciousness. As his eyes rested with a look of recognition on the dusky but familiar face of Cæsar, that devoted servant rolled his eyes upward and ejaculated:

"Bress de Lord! bress de Lord! Massa William, you's a gwine to get well," and the happy fellow wept tears of joy.

The wounded were in due time removed to the hospital in Washington, and our two heroes occupied adjacent beds. They were soon out of danger, though there was no prospect of their taking part in any further operations during that campaign.

Cæsar nursed them both with the utmost fidelity, and seemed never to tire of rendering them every service in his power. Night and day he was at hand whenever wanted, and his dark face shone with the light of joy whenever there appeared a decided improvement in the condition of his patients.

As the two friends began to convalesce, and they resumed the familiar intercourse of cadet life, the days passed pleasantly away and the last two years seemed an interval of dreams. To men of active temperament, life confined to the narrow limits, and jostled by the unpleasant associations of a hospital, has not many attractions; but they had only to shut their eyes and listen to each other's voices to be transported, in imagination, back to their old room at

Norwich; and these days of their recovery and the gradual return of strength were the happiest they had known since their parting at the University. It was the calm after the storm, and they experienced a quietude of spirit born of the serenity around them.

"That was a neat trick of yours, Tom, in leaving Richmond," remarked Wolfe one day.

"A Yankee trick, but hardly worth patenting," replied Lyon.

"The Yankee is an inventive animal."

"I guess you reckon rightly; but I can't see how any man, even a Georgian, could remain shut up in prison, as I was, without trying to discover some way of escape."

"In your situation at that time, the idea of escape would never have occurred to me."

"And I presume the idea of getting away from here has not entered your tropical brain; but if I were in your situation I should be revolving in my mind some plan to get across the Potomac."

"I never was good at getting out of a scrape, but I am first rate at getting into one. There is nothing of your Yankee cuteness in my composition; it isn't indigenous to the southern soil."

"It is handy though sometimes," said Tom.

"Extremely useful, I admit; I am glad there are a few Yankees in the world. Nobody but a Boston Yankee would ever have thought of catching the lightning, and nobody born out of New England would ever have dreamed of teaching it to talk.

"It's a pity your compatriots, or fellow rebels, don't share your admiration of the Yankee. I fear you are not an orthodox confederate."

"I lived too long in Vermont, I think. But tell me, how did you get out of Libby?"

"I dropped out."

"That was easy enough after you got on the outside, but how was that done?"

"I whittled out with a jack knife."

"I might have known it. A jack knife is implement enough for a Yankee, no matter what the job before him. It is a waste of money to purchase guns and ammunition for your troops. If they were only armed with jack knives they would whittle the Confederacy into shavings in a single campaign."

"It pains me, that I am not able truthfully to say something complimentary in return," said Lyon; but whither tends this flood of praise? Can I tell you anything more in regard to my escape from your delightful country? Would you hear the narrative of my wanderings? It is another Odyssy.

"I would hear how it is that I find a piece of my property, called Cæsar, in your possession."

"Well, replied Lyon, beginning to suspect that his friend had some knowledge of the assistance he had received in leaving rebeldom. "I fell in with Cæsar after I had vacated my apartment at Libby, and as he expressed a desire to travel and see the world and to give a finishing touch to his education, I took him under my protection, and brought him with me to the United States. If you wish to regain your property, we have a fugitive slave law."

"I don't think I shall avail myself of it. I am glad to find Cæsar here. But I have been in Richmond, Tom, since you left it so suddenly."

"You have—and how is—did you find your people well?—Miss Heloise is the only one of your family that I have the honor to know."

"All quite well, thank you. My sister told me something of her intercourse with yourself and your fellow-prisoner and tried to make me think, Tom, that your escape was a surprise to her. I did not question her much.

not caring to develop a case of treason in my family, and allowed her to think that I believed what she wished to have me."

. "She may have suspected my intention to escape, but I never divulged it to her, as I did not wish either to lead her into treason, as you call it, or to impose upon her the performance of what she might esteem the painful yet imperative duty to betray me."

"Betray you! I truly believe my sister would sell the whole Confederacy and give away all my niggers, to help a certain friend of mine out of difficulty."

"Your frankness, Bill, deserves to be reciprocated. I assure you that I regard my capture on the peninsula as the most fortunate event of my life, since it brought me acquainted with Heloise. I admire and respect her as the embodiment of all the higher graces and virtues of her sex. I feel that I am all unworthy of her, and that it is asking much of your friendship to ask you, as I do, to smile upon my suit; but a man in love is always unreasonable."

"You have my hearty good wishes, old friend, and my full consent to call me brother. And now, since we understand each other, in this matter, I wish to ask you what has become of our friend Condon, the gigantic and heroic."

"As I told you at Richmond, he left the University to attend medical lectures at Albany, but I have not seen him since. He wrote me two or three times, each time telling of some astounding cure which he had just performed. He talked learnedly of the arterial system, mentioning by name as I remember, and thus showing his familiarity with the subject, the aorta and the auxiliary and brachial arteries. Penetrating still deeper, he spoke of the parietal bone, the clavicle, humerus, carpus and metacarpus, phalanges, femur, tibia and fibula. It was my fault, I suppose, that the correspondence was not kept up."

"You didn't appreciate his learning. What disgusted you would have been rich food for me. Mat approached nearer to my conception of Falstaff than any other person I ever met. He is probably now the mighty man in some small village; overtopping and overawing the multitude; slaying every third patient and laying the blame on Providence."

"No doubt," said Lyon; "and with his evening pipe he tells to gaping admirers in the village grocery tales of cadet life in which he figures as hero. He tells how at one time he fought and conquered, singlehanded, a score of Darties, and how on another occasion he saved two friends of his, Wolfe and Lyon, from a beating and brought them off unhurt."

While the two sick men were enjoying a feeble laugh over this picture of the imagination, a heavy step was heard approaching. A gruff voice came to their ears and turning their eyes to the quarter from which it came, they both gazed for some moments in speechless astonishment.

CHAPTER XI.

DR. CONDON AND HIS TWO PATIENTS—WOLFE EXCHANGED—AID AND COMFORT TO THE ENEMY—LYON JOINS HIS REGIMENT AT FAIRFAX COURT HOUSE—BRUSHING THE DUST OF A CENTURY FROM THE RECORDS OF THE COURT—UNCLE SAM VS. J. DAVIS ET. AL.

"AM I awake?" inquired Wolfe, rubbing his eyes and looking again. "And if awake, is the figure I see the air-drawn form of a disordered mind, or flesh and blood reality?"

"It is he, replied Lyon. "Hide your face partially and observe his motions. I think we will surprise him when he reaches us."

Down the long alley came the burly form of no other than Dr. Mat. Condon. Stopping here and there at the beds on either hand, he examined with a wise look the hurts of the occupants, asked a few questions, and gave some directions to the nurse in attendance, with a tone and manner which implied that a strict following of his directions would insure a recovery in every case.

Approaching the place where his friends lay in ambush for him, he stopped and turned first to Lyon.

"Well, my man, how are you to-day?" he inquired in a cheerful tone.

"Poorly, poorly, doctor," replied Lyon in a faint voice.

"What is your difficulty?"

"Sarcophagus of the cerebellum."

"Eh—what—"

"He's got it bad," came from the opposite bed.

"But *he* has got something worse" said Lyon with his face still concealed and nodding his head in Wolfe's direction.

"I'd like to know what it is!" exclaimed Dr. Condon, in some amazement.

"The poor fellow has the secession cerebropathy in its worst form."

"Hard cases," said the doctor; brought on by wounds, I suppose."

"Say 'induced' and I'll agree with you."

"We were shot all to pieces and just sewed together again. They brought the pieces here in a hand-basket, and the surgeon stitched one of that fellow's legs on to me by mistake," said the sufferer from cerebropathy.

Condon began to think he had a couple of madmen to deal with.

"Let me see your wound," he said to Lyon.

"Look, then," exclaimed his old comrade, uncovering his face and smiling at the puzzled Mat.

"Tom Lyon! you rascal, I've a mind to break the shell of your cerebellum."

"It's your only chance, Mat, I'm weak, now."

"And this other villian, must be Bill Wolfe," said Condon, turning to the other patient and exposing his features.

There was a laugh in which Condon joined heartily.

"Well, Boys' he said. "I'm glad to see you," and he shook their hands with fervor. "The reunion of three gallant hearts after a lapse of years is a joyous event. How we are pushed about on the checker board of life—few of us ever getting into the king-row, after all our jumping. But it is all for the best, boys, all for the best. What a lucky thing that I studied medicine, instead of entering the army, as all my inclinations urged me. In deference to a mother's tears, I forsook the path of glory to learn the healing art, and now I am qualified to do service to my dearest friends. Thank your stars, my wounded Cæsars, that I have found you. Now I'll have you out of this in less time than—"

"Do you mean to murder us, that you talk of getting us out of here?" interrupted Wolfe. "Your patients go out in boxes, I suppose."

"That's what he means," chimed in Lyon, "but they don't call it murder; that is a legal term. The medical profession has a variety of technical terms to designate different modes of snapping the vital thread."

"Their little pellets are more deadly than poisoned bullets, and what makes the doctors more terrible than an army with banners is the fact that their raw recruits are their best shots."

"Halt, there," cried Condon: "as a physician, as well as a soldier and a gentleman, I can't hear the profession slandered. If you don't give it the honor due, I leave you to your fate."

"We can't spare you, Mat, now we have you, but we can your medicine. You may safely reckon that we won't deplete your stock of drugs."

"No," added Lyon; "though willing to do almost anything to oblige an old friend, we are hardly ready to be made subjects of for the sake of furthering your knowledge and increasing your skill."

"I would like to show you how neatly I could take off your leg."

"We will take it for granted that you could do it very neatly."

"Well" said Condon, philosophically, "I suppose the doctors must be satisfied to remain to the end of time the unthanked benefactors of the race. Here I have left a lucrative practice and come on here, at the call of suffering humanity, but not a man is willing to submit to an operation, and if one has a limb taken off in an artistic manner, he looks upon the surgeon as a personal enemy."

"In mercy to your home patients," we ought to give you work enough to keep you here a few weeks said Wolfe.

And so the conversation went on. It was renewed every day when Condon visited the hospital, and though his prescriptions were ridiculed by his two patients, his cheerful company proved a cordial to them, and they daily grew better. They were soon able to walk about and Lyon began to think of rejoining his regiment.

Condon expressed to him the great desire he felt to seize the weapons of warfare and serve through the remainder of the war; but stated, at the same time, that the numerous and urgent letters which he received from his deserted patients and the pathetic letters of his aged mother left him no choice in the matter; he would be obliged to go home.

He did go, a few days before Lyon left the city, protesting to the last against the fate which doomed him to physical inaction while his whole soul was in arms.

About this time Wolfe was exchanged and when he departed for the Confederacy, Lyon gave him a letter addressed to Heloise, and divided with him the amount of greenbacks of which he happened at that time to be possessed.

"Aid and comfort to the enemy." said Lyon.

"I will leave you Cæsar as security," answered Wolfe, and clasping each others' hands for a moment. the two friends separated.

Maj. Lyon found his regiment quartered at Fairfax Court House, where he was welcomed by Dr. Safford and the rest of his old comrades. among whom was Lieutenant Joe. who had reported himself as fit for duty again.

There were some weeks of rest and quiet while waiting for the opening of the spring campaign, and our friends managed to pass the time agreeably.

Dr. Safford explored the archives and discovered many ancient documents and interesting records which he read and commented on to his companions.

One day he found the time colored papers relating to a suit on book-account. It appeared therefrom that in the year 1759 "Mr. John Stone, in account with Alexander Henderson, Factor for Mr. John Glassford," purchased sundry articles, among which were one pound powder, one ounce thread, two pounds sugar, one bushel salt, one pound brimstone, two dozen metal buttons, one pewter dish, two porringers, two quarts rum and one Testament, and neglected to pay therefor.

Mr. Glassford, after waiting a reasonable time, petitioned "the worshipful court of Fairfax" and prayed judgment for "four pounds, twelve shillings and five pence," with costs. Thereupon was issued the following summons:

"George the third by the grace of God of great Britain, France and Ireland, King, Defender of the Faith, etc., to the sheriff of Fairfax, Greeting: we command you that you summon John Stone to appear before our Justice of our said county court at the court-house the third Tuesday in next month to answer the petition of John Glassford, and have then and there this writ. Witness, Peter Wagner, clerk of our said court, the 30th day of April, in the 3d year of our Reign 1763.   P. WAGNER."

This was written as we have given it, on coarse paper, but in a fair round hand, as plain as print, and decidedly superior to the Spencerian hand, if legibility is the chief thing to be desired in writing.

Judgment was confessed by John Stone for the amount claimed,

"This case was brought before this worshipful court one hundred years ago," said Dr Safford, turning his mental eye backward over the course of time.

"And the sugar and the salt and the rum were used up long ago," said Hank.

"Yes, but the pewter dish may yet survive to plague us in the developed form of rebel bullets," remarked Lieut. Joe.

"History repeats itself, they say," continued the doctor, "and it appears to me that there is now a parallel case before this worshipful court. The descendants of this John Stone, defendant, stand charged on the books of Uncle Sam with having received from him sundry goods, benefits and blessings, for which they refuse to pay. Uncle Sam has petitioned to the supreme court of the country, in which every man sits as one of the Justices, and a summons has been issued and placed in the hands of Sheriff Grant to be served."

"And we are a part of the *posse comitatus* to help him serve it," said Lyon.

"I hope, said Merritt, "that the defendants will confess judgement with costs."

"They seem inclined to contest the case, said the major, "and we shall be obliged to employ the *argumentum vaculinum* in order to gain our cause."

"Yes, we will back them down, and now this court will take a recess and the possy come-at-us can do as it pleases," and private Wait, justice, rose from his seat and walked out with the dignity of a hundred years ago.

CHAPTER XII.

THE BATTLE OF THE WILDERNESS—CHARGE OF THE OLD BRIGADE—GRANT'S REPORT—BEHIND THE LOG BREASTWORK—THE FALL OF LYON—CÆSAR'S REPORT.

ULYSSES S. GRANT was made Lieutenant General, March 2d, 1864, and placed in command of all the armies of the United States. The army of the Potomac, numbering now something over 100,000 men, was divided into three corps, commanded respectively by Gens. Hancock, Warren and Segdwick—all being under the command of Gen. Meade. It crossed the Rapidan, May 4th, and moved into "The Wilderness." On Thursday, May 5th, the Vermont Brigade, which had crossed the river at Germania Ford the day before, met the rebel advance a short distance from the crossings. They met in the dense woods at close quarters and the battle of the Wilderness began.

The rebels had the advantage of position and rained their bullets in showers on the Old Brigade, which, however, stood firm. It held the key of the position of the whole army, and though its ranks were being terribly thinned, no man thought of retreating. The Vermonters repulsed every attempt to dislodge them, but their valor cost them 1,000 brave officers and men. That night they slept upon the battle field, with the dead bodies of their comrades around them, and the groans of the wounded and dying filling the air.

The next morning the Brigade advanced again to the attack, and fought with the same stern courage as on the day before, and still on the morning of the 7th they were ready for the conflict, but a slight skirmish demonstrated the fact that the enemy had retired from their front, and they contented themselves with capturing a large number of muskets which the enemy had collected.

The Brigade marched all night of May 7th, and the next day was sent again into the thickest of the fight. The 9th was spent in skirmishing and in fortifying a position under fire.

On the 10th, three regiments of the Brigade, under the command of our hero, now promoted to the rank of Colonel, formed part of a column ordered to charge the enemy's works. The Vermonters were the rear line of the charging column. The front lines met with partial success, gaining the works and capturing some prisoners, but were finally driven back by the enemy.

The rear line then advanced under a galling fire.

"The Old Brigade is wanted now!" cried Lyon to his men. "Forward! and take those works and hold them."

"Take your baggage with you; we go to stay," said Lieutenant Joe to his company.

"My trunk is checked," put in Hank, as a rousing cheer rang out from the lines.

Forward they plunged with a resistless energy. Men fell, but the column moved onward. Nothing but death could stop them. Over the works they sprang, driving out the enemy at the point of the bayonet. They planted their tattered colors there and greeted them with hearty cheers.

But they were not allowed to hold undisputed possession of the works. The enemy made desperate attempts to retake them, but again and again were beaten off by the obstinate defenders who were determined to hold and occupy what they had won, if it were only with their dead bodies.

"We've moved in here with our goods and shan't move out till next April, unless we've a mind to," remarked private Wait to the hindmost of the retreating rebels, who had charged the ranks in vain.

"If we like the premises and pay our rent, there's no law to compel us. We're a quiet family, too, if you let us alone."

The position, however, was judged untenable by the general in command of the movement, and orders were sent to the Vermonters to withdraw from the ranks and fall back.

"Ridiculous!" muttered private Wait, as he heard the order, but speaking to a soldier on his right, who happened to be his uncle, Joseph Dickinson.

"By golly, I think so," returned the uncle.

"I like the place, uncle Joseph, and I am going to stay here. If you go, you can tell my ma'am and Catherine, where you left me."

"Can't we hold it, Colonel?" inquired Lieut. Safford.

"We are doing it and we can," answered Lyon.

"Then don't order us back."

"I won't if I can help it."

"Tell the General," he said to the waiting aid, "that we can hold the works for six months, if supplied with rations and ammunition."

Again the rebs swept up to regain their lost works, and again a withering fire of musketry, from men who wasted few bullets, drove them back in disorder.

But soon thereafter, the Vermonters, in obedience to a positive order from the General, were obliged to retire from the ground they had so bravely won and obstinately held on to.

The next morning, Gen. Grant sent to the War Department the following dispatch:

"HEADQUARTERS IN THE FIELD,
   May 11th, 1864—8 A. M.

We have now ended the sixth day of very heavy fighting. The result, to this time, is much in our favor.

Our losses have been heavy as well as of the enemy. I think the loss of the enemy must be greater.

We have taken over 5,000 prisoners by battle, whilst he has taken from us but few, except stragglers.

I propose to fight it out on this line, if it takes all summer.

U. S. GRANT, Lt. Gen. commanding
   the Armies of the U. S."

On the 11th day of May, the Brigade was constantly under fire, and on the 12th it was ordered to support Hancock, and was engaged in one of the hardest fights which it had yet experienced. The Brigade was under the command of Gen. Lewis A. Grant. A breastwork of logs and rails only separated it from the enemy.

The combatants fired into each other's faces, and fought with clubbed muskets and even pieces of fence rails, in a hand-to-hand struggle as they alternately made or repelled assaults.

Crouching down behind the breastworks, they would load, and then rising quickly, discharge their muskets at the enemy and fall down again as quickly to the ground.

Hank, who was fighting on his own hook, rose to fire just as a squad of the enemy rose for the same purpose. Ducking suddenly as he saw the position, their bullets went over his head.

"You're immensely careless," he exclaimed reproachfully, as he quickly rose again and sent his bullet through the shoulder of a dropping rebel.

A yell of pain attested the effect of his shot.

A reinforcement of the enemy came up now, and, with frightful yells, they mounted the breastwork, some of them even jumping down on to our side, in the attempt to dislodge the Old Brigade.

"Drive them back!" cried Lyon, as he himself set an example to his men.

Screams, shouts and groans made an indescribable tumult as North met South in a trial of physical strength.

Those whose pieces were loaded fired them in the faces of the assailants and then turned them end for end, dealing their blows right and left. Swords and bayonets met as officers and men mingled in an indiscriminate combat. Clubs were wielded with the dexterity of those whose favorite weapon is a stick of blackthorn.

Lieut. Joe, seizing a long rail in his hands, swung it around with such tremendous force that he swept a rank of rebels from the breastwork, like so many chickens from a hen-roost.

"That's Uncle Abe's weapon" said Hank; "swinging it once more, and the battle is over."

"If your rail had been a little longer, Lieutenant," said Lyon, "you would have knocked the brains out of the whole Confederacy."

Those of the enemy who had got over the breastwork were made prisoners. Those on the works jumped back to their own side.

"After them!" shouted Lyon, springing upon the breastwork, followed by his men.

"It's no more than polite to return their call," said Hank, as he leaped down among his late guests.

The rebels by scores threw down their arms and surrendered themselves.

With their prisoners, the Vermonters retreated to their own side of the log fence just in time to escape from, and be ready to meet, another flood of Southern chivalry, which was dashed up against the works they defended.

Occasionally a white flag was shown on the other side, and as our fire slackened the confederates swarmed over and voluntarily gave themselves up.

But others were led up to take their places, and the contest was continued. Thus for eight hours the Brigade was engaged, and not without loss, though it inflicted greater loss on the enemy.

Lyon's coat was perforated by balls, but he received no wound. Hank had the heel shot off his boot as he stood on the breastwork. Lieut. Safford was carried to the rear, wounded.

Late in the day, Col. Lyon thought he saw an opportunity, by a sudden charge, in force, of capturing a large number of the enemy. The word was accordingly passed along, weapons were prepared and at a given signal the Vermonters poured once more over the breastwork like a spring-freshet over the dam across a mountain stream. The movement was highly successful at first. The enemy yielded before the impetuous assault, large numbers were captured and hurried to the Union side of the fence; but our friends were not to escape with impunity.

Two rebel regiments came to the rescue of their friends and charged our troops in turn, forcing them back in spite of their best efforts It was the fiercest encounter of the day.

Lyon gave the order to retire, but fought himself in the the rear of his retreating command to enable it to do so in good order. The enemy pressed closer and at length broke our line. There was a confused struggle for a moment—a discharge of small arms at close quarters, and Lyon throwing up his hands wildly, cried out—

"I have got it!"

He fell senseless to the ground. There was a rush of

the enemy over his motionless body, and his men were driven over the breakworks. There they halted and held their own, but they were not able to regain the ground they had left nor recover the body of their commander.

Till after dark the Brigade defended the position, but there were many sad hearts at the loss of Lyon. In the evening the men were marched around, feeling their way through the dense woods to the extreme right, where they took position for the night.

Dr. Safford, as soon as he found time, sought out private Wait to inquire after the colonel.

"You think he was killed, do you Hank?"

"Yes, I have no doubt of it," replied Hank with a tremor in his voice. "I stood close beside him; a pistol bullet from a rebel captain, who won't ever shoot another Yankee, struck him in the breast and he fell as I've seen many a dead man fall."

"Didn't move or speak again?"

"No; but of course I didn't stay there long; we were driven back in a hurry, you know."

"He is probably dead," said the doctor, with a sigh. "The only wonder is that he was not killed long ago. So reckless of danger has he been."

For the next three days the Brigade was not engaged.

Cæsar's grief was inconsolable when he heard of Col. Lyon's death. He felt that his mission was accomplished, and he would gladly have returned to his mistress if he had known of any safe way of doing so. Under the exciting circumstances, he determined to write, trusting to chance to forward his communication. After spending the most of one day on his epistle, he submitted it to Hank to whom he had attached himself after the loss of his master. It was written phonetically, or as Hank said, niggeretically as follows:

"Mi deer missis—ize bery sory to tel yer de bad nuze

spees yer wanter heer do massa wilyum dum got kotched bi de yankis i found him mos ded an nust him till he conwalesscntid an went bac to our side to kil hisself ober agin mass lium was kild 2 free times fitiall de time neber seed de likes an now heze ded mis holoeze ize fraid i neber get outer dis don't kotch me in anoder scrap whar bullets is mity site mor plenty dan hokakes hopin yer wel ize mos superflewously yer distingwisht and obejunt survant. Seezur."

Strange as it may seem, this letter, which Hank undertook to deliver in order to satisfy the writer and which he fastened to a tree, was afterwards found by Col. Wolfe and forwarded to its destination.

CHAPTER XIII.

FROM THE WILDERNESS TO COLD HARBOR—IN THE SHENANDOAH VALLEY—RETURN TO PETERSBURG—THE CAMPAIGN OF 1865—THE OLD BRIGADE MAKES A BEGINNING OF THE END—CAPTURE OF PETERSBURG AND RICHMOND—LEE'S RETREAT—COL. WOLFE A PRISONER—THE LAST CHARGE OF THE CONFEDERACY—LEE'S SURRENDER—THE UNION SAVED.

N the 16th operations were renewed by a reconnoisance in the direction of Spotsylvania Court House, a part of the Brigade gallantly driving the enemy's skirmishers to their main line of works. On the 18th the Vermonters with the rest of the 6th corps and the 2d corps charged under heavy artillery fire and held the front line until ordered to retire.

From Spottsylvania the Brigade marched on the night of the 21st to Guinea's Station, thence to the North Anna River, which they crossed and re-crossed, skirmishing with the enemy and tearing up the railroad. On the 27th it crossed the Pamunkey River. On the 29th it turned toward Richmond, being almost every day engaged either in marching or fighting, and on the first of June the gallant remnant of the old Brigade arrived at Cold Harbor, its total losses during this bloody month of May, from the Rapidan to Cold Harbor, footing up nearly 2,000 men.

P

But neither their toils nor their dangers were over. As soon as they arrived they were thrown into battle on the extreme left, towards the Chickahominy, and for twelve days they were under an incessant fire of musketry and artillery. On the 3d of June they were posted in the edge of the woods, with no protection but the trees, and kept up a sort of Indian warfare for a while.

With the Vermonters here was Col. Ewart's regiment and that of Maj. Staples. These two officers, thus brought together, recognized each other and renewed their former acquaintance. Merritt (now Major) was in command of his regiment, and he with Dr. Safford and private Wait made all of our old friends still left in arms.

As the muskets cracked and men fell here and there, or the bark flew from the trees, without any material advantage being gained by either side, Ewarts began to chafe at the desultory fighting, and expressed his preference for sharper and closer work.

"Go out Colonel, alone, like Goliah" said Staples and dare the rebel host to battle, as you did once on a time the Dartmouth boys."

"I should rather go out to meet their Goliah," returned the Colonel: "I think I should like that better than biding here behind a tree."

"I pity the giant's coat, if you get hold of him."

"We will soon strip the coat from the whole Confederacy, and show the world what a skeleton it is."

In another quarter Hank was alternately firing and talking with the utmost rapidity, and if his words failed to hit the mark his bullets were better aimed.

"I never saw such an unreasonable set as those rebels, did you, Uncle Joseph?" inquired Hank of his relative, who stood behind the nearest tree.

"No, nephew, I didn't—least-ways I disremember to."

"No argument but lead is heavy enough to convince

them," continued Hank, discharging his piece with evident effect.

"Now, I've been nearly three years," he said, loading as he spoke, "trying to persuade these fellows to support our good government. I've stopped some of them from opposing it—"

Here he fired again with effect, by way of parenthesis, and immediately proceeded to reload.

"But those that are left are just as unreasonable as ever. They act like a country district school meeting, which always goes to work to defeat what it pretends to want."

Here he fired again.

"They say they want a good government, and here they are trying to tear down the best government that ever existed."

"Exactly," assented Uncle Joseph.

"I don't know of any other way of doing it except this"—and here he fired twice in succession without speaking. This method of argument was certainly forcible. It made some impression, and was the only one likely to be appreciated by his opponents.

The Brigade was finally withdrawn from this position and sent to another part of the field.

About midnight on the night of the 12th, the Brigade started on the march for Petersburg by the way of Charles City Court House, and arrived there on the afternoon of the 17th.

It is not our purpose to detail minutely the operations of the Army of the Potomac, or even all those in which the Brigade was specially engaged. We shall note only the more remarkable and memorable events, and those in which our characters were concerned.

The Brigade was actively employed in the neighborhood of Petersburg till the 9th of July, when it embarked at City point for Washington, and during the remainder of the summer and fall served against the rebel marauders and other forces scattered through northern Virginia. To it belonged the honor of victoriously beginning "the series of splendid movements and successive battles which drove the rebel forces from the Valley of Shenandoah."

The times of enlistment of most of the regiments expired in July, but many men re-enlisted and these with new recruits kept up the organizations.

Meanwhile, Grant kept hammering away persistently at Petersburg, and striking at Lee's army wherever and whenever he could hit it, while Sheridan was running amuck through the Valley, hitting at every organized form of rebellion, and devastating the country so that it might not again attract the enemy into it.

The campaign of 1864 ended the latter part of October with the battle of Boyden Plank Road, brought on by a general advance of Grant's forces, and with Sheridan's brilliant snatching of victory from defeat after his twenty mile ride from Winchester. The Old Brigade was with him and gained new laurels in that double battle.

The winter passed away without any movement of importance in Virginia. Grant was content to hold Lee's army in his neighborhood and prevent it from operating elsewhere. There were a few rebel raids in northern Virginia but they were of little consequence and had no appreciable effect upon the result of the war. The Old Brigade returned to the army in front of Petersburg about the middle of December and went into winter quarters.

Gen. Sheridan, acting under the command of Gen. Grant, opened the campaign of 1865 by a cavalry raid aimed at Lynchburg. He left Winchester Feb. 27th with 10,000 mounted men. Hurling himself against the rebel Gen. Early, intrenched at Waynesboro, he gained a complete victory, leaving little of Early's force except Early himself. The First Regiment Vermont Cavalry formed a part of Sheridan's force and participated in the dangers and glories of the expedition.

Grant issued his order for a general advance of his left, the latter part of March, and on the 29th, the 5th and 2d corps moved out southwesterly to co-operate with Sheridan, who, coming down the valley, had now arrived at the grand scene of action where the final struggle of the Rebellion was to be made.

The main body of the army still remained in the trenches before Petersburg to bombard or assault the town and ready to enter it upon its evacuation by the enemy, while Gen. Weitzel threatened Richmond with a considerable force from the north of the James.

On Saturday, April 1st, Lee's right wing was demolished, and as darkness fell, the guns before Petersburg opened from right to left, and with tongues of fire thundered forth the doom of the beseiged city.

At daybreak on Sunday morning an assault was ordered. The Vermont Brigade, with the Sixth Corps under Wright, charged and drove everything before them up to the Boyden road. Wheeling to the left, toward Hatcher's Run, they swept down the rear of the rebel intrenchments, capturing many guns and several thousand prisoners.

The honor of being the first to break the enemy's line is claimed by the Vermont Brigade. The first colors planted on the works belonged to the Brigade, and the first man to mount the works was Capt. Gould, of the Fifth regiment.

Gen. L. A. Grant was wounded, and the command of the Brigade devolved on Lieut.-Colonel Tracy of the Second regiment.

The enemy broke and fled in every direction. The Brigade lost all organization in the ardor of pursuit. Officers and men vied with each other in a four mile race after the fugitive rebels.

"My kingdom for a horse!" cried Hank, as he panted

along. "I never before fully appreciated the convenience of long legs and a spare body. These fellows run like hounds."

And you like a turtle," said Maj. Merritt, as he dashed past.

Gen. Meade speaks of this attack of the Sixth Corps, as "the decisive movement of the campaign."

President Davis, in Richmond, was at church that morning when the dispatch from Gen. Lee was handed to him:

"My lines are broken in three places. Richmond must be evacuated this evening."

Petersburg was evacuated that afternoon and Richmond the next morning.

Sunday evening the Brigade established its headquarters at the Turnbull House, where Gen. Lee had had his headquarters during the winter.

Early the next morning the Old Brigade, with the Sixth Corps, started in rapid pursuit of the rebel army, which was now intent only on getting away.

Gen. Weitzel at 6 A. M., of the same day, entered the burning city of Richmond, which had been set on fire by the retreating rebels, and the American flag soon floated once more in the breeze above the Capitol of Virginia, and was greeted with enthusiastic cheers by the excited multitude below.

Petersburg was occupied the same day by our troops, who marched proudly and unopposed into the city they had struggled for so long.

On the afternoon of the 6th the sixth corps came up with the enemy at Sailor's Creek and an engagement ensued. A portion of Sheridan's cavalry, by a bold charge, cut off the rebel Gen. Ewell's corps from the rest of Lee's army and inclosed it between them and the advancing 6th corps. The trapped Confederates fought with the courage of desperation, but they fought without a chance of victory or escape.

Col. Wolfe with his regiment found himself between the jaws of the Union vise and dashed into the fight with all the recklessness of his nature.

"Death, but not surrender! Georgians, follow me!" he cried, and rushed forward to meet the stern charge of our Sixth Corps.

But the Confederates were discouraged by the hopeless nature of their situation, and threw down their arms and surrendered. Ewell himself, with four other generals, were among the 6,000 prisoners taken this day. Col. Wolfe was captured, foaming with rage at what he called the cowardice of his men. He was courteously received by Major Merritt, and soon meeting with several former friends, among whom were Staples and Ewarts, and finding Cæsar overjoyed to see him again alive and unhurt, he seemed to grow reconciled to his fate and to that of the Confederacy.

"Ize mighty glad to see you Massa William" said the faithful black with tears in his eyes. "I neber let you leabe me agin. Ize yer nigga and does't want no freedom. Massa Linkum's mancerpation no use to Cæsar."

On the night of April 5th, many prominent rebel officers met around a bivouac fire to discuss the situation, and unanimously agreed that a capitulation was inevitable. Lee was not present, but his opinion must have coincided with theirs, for during the 7th and 8th, though making every effort to escape the toils of his foe, he was engaged in a correspondence with Grant looking towards a surrender of his army.

On the morning of Sunday the 9th, however, the rebel chief thought he saw one remaining chance and determined to improve it. Sheridan had intercepted his flight and presuming that his way was blocked by cavalry alone, he ordered a charge of infantry. It was made and it proved the last charge of that gallant army, which had fought, with a courage seldom surpassed, from the time of the first Bull Run till then, when a mere wreck of its former self, it was surrounded by foes in overwhelming numbers.

Sheridan's dismounted troopers retired slowly before their advance for a while, but suddenly "the horsemen moved swiftly to the right and dismounted, revealing lines of solid infantry in battle array, before whose wall of gleaming bayonets the astonished enemy recoiled in blank despair." Before our cavalry had time to charge them the Confederates waved a white flag and hostilities were at once suspended.

That day, Lee surrendered his army of about 27,000, where its flight had been stopped, about nineteen miles from Lynchburg. For this purpose, Grant and Lee met at the house of Mr. W. McLean, near Appomattox Court House, and in a brief interview settled the terms of surrender.

The rebellion was virtually ended, though not for some weeks after did Johnston surrender to Sherman, and the other rebel armies disband or surrender. As the glad tidings spread with the speed of lightning over the loyal North, rejoicings were everywhere indulged in that the blood and treasure had not been spent in vain, but had purchased this glorious result—the Union saved and Liberty preserved!

CHAPTER XIV.

COL. WOLFE PAROLED AND WITH CÆSAR SETS OUT FOR HOME—SPIRITUAL RECONSTRUCTION—A HAPPY MEETING AND SURPRISE—CÆSAR SEES A GHOST—AN EXPLANATION—COL. LYON REJOINS THE BRIGADE—HOMEWARD MARCH AND MUSTER OUT—UNION BY MARRIAGE—LAW FIRM OF LYON AND WOLFE.

THE Vermont Brigade was at Farmville, guarding supplies, at the time of Lee's surrender. From there they marched to Burkesville Junction where they remained two weeks, and here Col. Wolfe, having been paroled, took leave of the Vermonters and, taking Cæsar with him, set out for home, or rather towards the place where he expected to find his sister.

A long time previous to Lee's surrender he had foreseen that Richmond was not likely to continue a desirable place of residence, and probably not a safe one, and he had cordially seconded his sister's plan to take up her abode with an aunt living in a retired part of the state, remote from railroads and routes likely to be pursued by hostile parties. Here Heloise had quietly remained during the past year, and all the more contentedly because her aunt, a widow lady, was of her way of thinking in regard to the merits of secession. Twice her brother had visited her, and she was never a very long time without hearing from him.

Procuring a couple of horses, the Colonel and Cæsar started on their journey, and as they passed by the evidences that the Confederacy was a thing of the past, and the cause a "lost cause" indeed, Wolfe reviewed in his mind the history of the last four years, and found reason to regret the part which he, in company with others, had taken in the effort to dismember the American republic. His secession fever was rapidly abating, and as his eyes met here and there the old flag of the Union, floating like sections of sunset cloud in the air, his heart swelled with an irrepressible feeling of pride that it was the flag of his country, and he experienced a sense of joy that his arm was free once more to battle beneath its folds and for its glory. In spirit he was "reconstructed."

The two proceeded at good pace for most of the time, for they had a long ride before them; but occasionally they slackened their speed, and master and servant (in reality free and equal fellow-citizens as Wolfe could not help remembering) fell into conversation to relieve the monotony of the way.

"Well, Cæsar, how do you like the Yankees? You ought to know something about them by this time."

"Berry well, massa, if you do—jes' as you say."

"Were they kind to you?"

"Treated me like a brodder."

"Was Col. Lyon a good master?"

"Next to you, massa William. He neber let no harm come to Cæsar till he got killed."

"He is dead, then, is he?" said Wolfe with a strange expression of face, which his sable attendant could not read.

"Yis, massa; shot right froo de heart, dey said. I werren't dere."

"No, I'll warrant you. No danger of you ever being shot, Cæsar."

"Hope's not, massa."

They rode on again in silence, Wolfe evidently being busy with his own thoughts, and Cæsar knowing better than to speak when not spoken to.

At noon they stopped at a little tavern and refreshed themselves and horses, after which they pushed on again. At nightfall they had not reached their destination, but Wolfe was familiar with the road and he kept on.

About nine o'clock in the evening they saw before them the glimmering lights of a mansion house, situated in a retired locality several miles distant from any habitation. Urging their tired steeds to a slight increase of speed, they soon rode up to and dismounted at the door.

A swarm of negroes, lately enfranchised, but ignorant of the fact, quickly surrounded them and took their horses, while they gave the Colonel, as soon as they recognized him, an affectionate welcome.

A medley of voices and expressions greeted his ear:

"Berry glad, sah—"

"Se, yer all alibe again, sah—"

"Hopes yer well massa Colonel—"

"Young missus be delighted—"

"Dis way, massa—"

"I tells de missis."

But there was no need of any announcement. The uproar outside brought the inmates of the mansion out on the veranda and Wolfe was soon shaking hands with his aunt, his sister, and a pale gentleman in civilian's dress.

"How are you Tom—getting stronger?" he said to the latter.

"Yes, I am; but what brings you here at this time?" replied the gentleman.

"I'll tell you soon, but come in now; I have a surprise in store."

"Here, Cæsar, I want you," he called, and that person soon appeared and followed his master into the house.

As the door closed and Cæsar stood cap in hand waiting for orders, the strange gentleman turned and looked earnestly at him.

Cæsar returned the look with interest. His eyes seemed starting from his head, while his teeth chattered audibly.

The gentleman smiled and advanced towards him saying—

"How are you, Cæsar?"

As Cæsar saw him approaching, he dashed for the door screaming—

"Lemme out! lemme out!"

But his master stood with his back to the door laughing at the poor fellow's fright.

"Do you think me a ghost, Cæsar?" inquired the object of his terror.

"I knows you's dead, massa Lyon, dey all said so."

While they enjoyed a laugh at this reply, Cæsar regained his self-possession, and was finally convinced of his mistake.

"I am happy to inform you that I am still alive and likely soon to be well," said Col. Lyon, for it was indeed he.

And now some explanation is due the reader as well as Cæsar.

In the fight on the rebel side of the log-breastwork in the Wilderness, Hank Wait supposed and reported that Lyon fell dead, or at least mortally wounded. But such was not the fact. The next morning, Col. Wolfe, who was always on the lookout for his friend, and who never passed a dead or wounded Federal officer without a searching look, found Lyon on the field desperately wounded and had him carefully conveyed to a place of safety. Knowing that if his friend was consigned to the mercy of the Confederacy and sent to Andersonville, or any other prison pen, he would surely die, and that nothing but the most tender care and nursing could save his life, he determined to exercise himself a little sovereign authority in the behalf of friendship. Accordingly, as soon as Lyon was able to stand the journey, he dispatched him with two faithful servants to the quiet residence of his aunt, feeling confident that kind lady and good Union woman and his sister Heloise would do their utmost for the wounded officer.

The event proved that he was not mistaken. Our hero, who was in a very critical situation for several months, was cared for with the greatest solicitude, and nothing that could minister to his comfort or contribute to his recovery was lacking. After he began to gain he was provided with a suit of plain clothes, his Federal uniform being put out of sight, and the servants and others were given to understand that he was a relative of the family from another southern State, who had come there for the improvement of his health.

His convalescence was slow, but could not fail to be pleasant, for beside the pleasure of feeling that his former strength was gradually returning, his days were spent in the society of her who, by her tireless devotion, had done so much to bring him back to life.

As the pleasant days of spring arrived to clothe the earth with verdure, and he was able to walk and ride with her, he felt a certain degree of that insanity which led Marc Antony to sell his glory for the smiles of woman. Nevertheless, he frequently yearned to return to the field of conflict, even before his health was sufficiently restored to render him fit to endure the hardships of active service. But his honor was pledged to Wolfe that he would not attempt to escape, and he therefore waited till his friend should release him from his promise, or he should be exchanged.

After Cæsar had satisfied himself of the reality of Lyon's existence in the flesh, and had expressed his great joy thereat, he was allowed to retire, and then Lyon inquired of his friend the cause of his unexpected visit.

"I come to tell you, Tom, that you are no longer my prisoner, but are at liberty to take up your line of march in whatever direction you please."—

"Thank you; but why—"

"The Confederacy is dead! Lee has surrendered! Richmond is taken! the war is ended!"

"Oh! what happy news!" said Heloise, while tears glistened in her eyes."

"Thank God!" exclaimed the old lady " that this cruel and wicked strife is over."

Lyon was at first too much surprised to speak, and when he found ability to speak, he hesitated to express the joy and triumph which he felt, out of regard to the possible feelings of his friend. Wolfe saw this and said :

"You may indulge yourself in three cheers if you like ; I don't feel so badly as you doubtless think."

"I am certainly pleased " said Lyon ; " I am surprised too, at the sudden completeness of the Union triumph, though the end is what I have always expected."

"Your chief regret is that you were not in at the death. You meant to charge the 'last ditch' in which the hunted Confederacy should ensconce itself. I know the naughtiness of your heart, Tom."

"Whatever my wishes, I was not there," replied Lyon, " but I suppose Vermont was represented."

"Yes, I left your Vermont heroes this morning at Burkesville Junction."

"And there I must join them."

In spite of the urgent requests to remain, Lyon determined to set out the next day. Before he retired that night, however, he won the consent of Heloise that he might soon return to claim her as his own.

Next morning, after an affectionate farewell to all, he started, being accompanied by Cæsar, who was sent to bring back the horses.

Arriving unheralded at the camp of the Vermont

Brigade, his old companions in arms exhibited almost as much surprise and alarm as Cæsar had done. Their first excitement over, however, they gave him as warm a welcome as he had reason to expect.

"It's a waste of time and tears to mourn for you, Colonel," said Hank. "We could have made a great saving if we had only known that bullets cannot hurt you."

"He must live to be President. It is written," said Dr. Safford solemnly.

On the 23d of April, the Brigade left the Junction and marched to Danville, 105 miles, in a few hours more than four days. From Danville they moved by railroad to Manchester, May 18th, and on the 24th marched for Washington, D. C. They went into camp near Munson's Hill, Va., and remained there until mustered out of service.

On the 7th of June, the Vermont Brigade was reviewed by Gov. Smith at Bailey's Cross Roads, Va., and on the 8th the Brigade with the rest of the Sixth Corps was reviewed by the President at Washington. On the 24th of June, Brevet-Major General L. A. Grant issued his final address to the brigade he had so long commanded, and on the 28th of June 1865, the Vermont Brigade, which had won for itself such lasting honor, ceased to exist as an organization. Its members returned to the various pursuits of private and civil life. Like streams which flow into and combine with the waters of the ocean, the returning volunteers flowed back to and mingled with their fellow-citizens of the republic, forming a homogeneous whole.

Major Merritt won fame and fortune by his musical talents. Capt. Nason invented a wonderful churn, and was successful in persuading the farmers to buy it. Maj. Staples studied law and is now a rising man in New Hampshire. Ewarts has been governor of one of the western states. Condon is in the patent medicine business, and if his advertisements are to be believed, it is the utmost folly for any one to die of any manner of disease whatever. Dr. Safford returned to the practice of his profession in a quiet town of Windham County, and still drives his gig along the shady mountain roads in summer, and his cutter over and through the snow drifts in winter, alleviating the distresses of his fellow creatures. By way of amusement he cultivates flowers in their season and indulges his literary taste without regard to the time of the year. His poem, "The Processsion of the Flowers," and some of his war-songs are productions of decided merit ; but though, like all poets, "fond of his own sweet songs," he is fain to confess that Vermont has as yet produced no poet superior to Homer. Private Hank Wait is tilling the paternal acres by proxy, and has more than regained the flesh he lost in his country's service.

Lieut. Joe Safford, twice wounded in battle, and enfeebled by hardship and exposure, returned home with a shattered constitution, and was not able to check the slow but determined advance of the enemy, death. Not as he would have chosen to die, in the excitement of battle, but quietly, in the midst of mourning friends, his spirit began its march eternal. His body rests in the little graveyard at Greeenbush, in the shadow of the beautiful mountain, which his feet in boyhood often climbed.

In the autumn of 1865, Col. Lyon went down to Virginia in the interests of union, but without any orders from government, and when he returned to Vermont he brought Heloise with him as his wife. Col. Wolfe continued at the South for a year or two, but finally yielded to the solicitations of his friend and his sister and came North to reside permanently. The Norwich Cadets entered into partnership in one of our most beautiful and thriving villages. About the door of their office Cæsar is generally to be observed in sunny weather. Above the door a sign is visible, inscribed "Lyon and Wolfe." The initial letters of these three words sufficiently declare the business done within, and the line beneath the names is hardly necessary, so well are our heroes known. Eight years and eight days have now passed since Lee's surrender, and the name of Col. Lyon is a prominent one in his native State. There is still time, and the prospect is fair that the prophecy of Dr. Safford will be fulfilled, and a Norwich Cadet become a tenant of the White House for at least four years. It is certainly time that Vermont should have a chance to try housekeeping there,

THE END,

www.ingramcontent.com/pod-product-compliance
Lightning Source LLC
Chambersburg PA
CBHW020102170426
43199CB00009B/366